CentOS High Availability

Leverage the power of high availability clusters on
CentOS Linux, the enterprise-class, open source
operating system

Mitja Resman

PUBLISHING

BIRMINGHAM - MUMBAI

CentOS High Availability

First published: April 2015

Production reference: 1220415

Published by Packt Publishing Ltd.
Livery Place
35 Livery Street
Birmingham B3 2PB, UK.

ISBN 978-1-78528-248-5

www.packtpub.com

Credits

Author
Mitja Resman

Reviewers
Denis Fateyev
Christophe Grenier

Commissioning Editor
Veena Pagare

Acquisition Editor
Reshma Raman

Content Development Editor
Neeshma Ramakrishnan

Technical Editor
Abhishek R. Kotian

Copy Editor
Vikrant Phadke

Project Coordinator
Danuta Jones

Proofreaders
Stephen Copestake
Safis Editing
Paul Hindle

Indexer
Rekha Nair

Production Coordinator
Melwyn D'sa

Cover Work
Melwyn D'sa

About the Author

Mitja Resman hails from a small, beautiful country called Slovenia in south-central Europe. He is a fan of Linux and also an open source enthusiast. He is a Red Hat Certified Engineer and Linux Professional Institute professional. Working as a system administrator, Mitja gained years of professional experience with open source software and Linux system administration on local and international projects. The Swiss Army Knife syndrome makes him an expert in the field of VMware virtualization, Microsoft system administration, and more recently, Android system administration.

Mitja has a strong desire to learn, develop, and share knowledge with others. This is the reason he started a blog called GeekPeek.Net. It provides CentOS Linux guides and how-to articles covering all sorts of topics appropriate for both beginners and advanced users. Mitja is also a devoted father and husband. His daughter and wife are the ones who take his mind off the geek stuff and make him appreciate life and look forward to the things to come.

I would like to thank my wife for putting up with my late night writing sessions and for all the support I got when I decided to write this book. I would also like to thank all of my family for the words of encouragement at the time of writing this book. Also, a special thanks to my friend who introduced me to Linux many years ago.

About the Reviewers

Denis Fateyev holds a Master's degree in Computer Science, and has been working with Linux for more than 10 years, mostly with Red Hat and CentOS. He currently works as a Perl programmer and a DevOps for a small German company. Being a keen participant in the open source community, he is a package maintainer in the Fedora and Repoforge projects. Foreign languages (German and Spanish) and linguistics are also his passion.

Denis can be reached at `denis@fateyev.com`.

Christophe Grenier holds a diploma from ESIEA Graduate School of Engineering, and is the director of operations at Global SP — a French IT service provider. He has more than 15 years of experience in Red Hat Linux systems. He uses the Corosync cluster solution from CentOS 5 onwards. Christophe teaches several courses about Linux and IT Security in Sécurité de l'Information et des Systèmes at ESIEA Mastère Spécialisé. He is also known for the open source data recovery utilities, TestDisk, and PhotoRec.

www.PacktPub.com

Support files, eBooks, discount offers, and more

For support files and downloads related to your book, please visit www.PacktPub.com.

Did you know that Packt offers eBook versions of every book published, with PDF and ePub files available? You can upgrade to the eBook version at www.PacktPub.com and as a print book customer, you are entitled to a discount on the eBook copy. Get in touch with us at service@packtpub.com for more details.

At www.PacktPub.com, you can also read a collection of free technical articles, sign up for a range of free newsletters and receive exclusive discounts and offers on Packt books and eBooks.

https://www2.packtpub.com/books/subscription/packtlib

Do you need instant solutions to your IT questions? PacktLib is Packt's online digital book library. Here, you can search, access, and read Packt's entire library of books.

Why subscribe?

- Fully searchable across every book published by Packt
- Copy and paste, print, and bookmark content
- On demand and accessible via a web browser

Free access for Packt account holders

If you have an account with Packt at www.PacktPub.com, you can use this to access PacktLib today and view 9 entirely free books. Simply use your login credentials for immediate access.

Table of Contents

Preface

The book will guide you through the process of installing, configuring, and administering a multinode computer cluster on CentOS version 6 and 7 using two different cluster suites with respect to the CentOS version.

What this book covers

Chapter 1, Getting Started with High Availability, provides facts about high availability.

Chapter 2, Meet the Cluster Stack on CentOS, shows you how cluster stack software works as a whole to provide high availability.

Chapter 3, Cluster Stack Software on CentOS 6, covers installation and configuration of cluster stack software on CentOS 6.

Chapter 4, Resource Manager on CentOS 6, teaches you how to manage your cluster resources and services with the RGManager resource manager on CentOS 6.

Chapter 5, Playing with Cluster Nodes on CentOS 6, explains how to manage and administer cluster nodes on CentOS 6.

Chapter 6, Fencing on CentOS 6, provides the details and recommendations on the quorum disk on CentOS 6.

Chapter 7, Testing Failover on CentOS 6, discovers cluster node fencing on CentOS 6.

Chapter 8, Two-node Cluster Considerations on CentOS 6, covers some final cluster failover tests on CentOS 6.

Chapter 9, Cluster Stack Software on CentOS 7, shows you how to install and configure cluster stack software on CentOS 7.

Chapter 10, Resource Manager on CentOS 7, teaches you how to manage your cluster resources and services with the Pacemaker resource manager on CentOS 7.

Chapter 11, Playing with Cluster Nodes on CentOS 7, explains how to manage and administer cluster nodes on CentOS 7.

Chapter 12, STONITH on CentOS 7, introduces the details and recommendations on quorum disk on CentOS 7.

Chapter 13, Testing Failover on CentOS 7, covers cluster node fencing, the so-called STONITH, on CentOS 7.

Chapter 14, Two-node Cluster Considerations on CentOS 7, provides some final cluster failover tests on CentOS 7.

What you need for this book

To closely follow the guides provided in this book, three virtual or physical machines with a working CentOS version 6 or 7 installation are required. The machines must have Internet connectivity to provide successful software installation, and local network connectivity to provide normal cluster operation.

Who this book is for

This book is targeted at system engineers and system administrators who want to upgrade their knowledge and skills in high availability, and want to learn how to practically achieve high availability with CentOS Linux. You are expected to have good knowledge of CentOS Linux and basic networking experience.

Conventions

In this book, you will find a number of text styles that distinguish between different kinds of information. Here are some examples of these styles and an explanation of their meaning.

Code words in text, database table names, folder names, filenames, file extensions, pathnames, dummy URLs, user input, and Twitter handles are shown as follows: "If you want to change this, edit the NTP configuration file in `/etc/ntp.conf`."

Any command-line input or output is written as follows:

```
[root@node-1 ~]# service ntpd start
[root@node-1 ~]# chkconfig ntpd on
```

New terms and **important words** are shown in bold. Words that you see on the screen, for example, in menus or dialog boxes, appear in the text like this: "Check the **Cluster Status** parameter to confirm that the cluster node was removed from the cluster configuration."

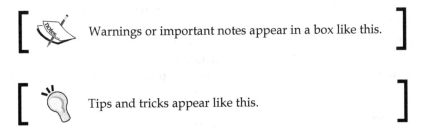

[Warnings or important notes appear in a box like this.]

[Tips and tricks appear like this.]

Reader feedback

Feedback from our readers is always welcome. Let us know what you think about this book—what you liked or disliked. Reader feedback is important for us as it helps us develop titles that you will really get the most out of.

To send us general feedback, simply e-mail feedback@packtpub.com, and mention the book's title in the subject of your message.

If there is a topic that you have expertise in and you are interested in either writing or contributing to a book, see our author guide at www.packtpub.com/authors.

Customer support

Now that you are the proud owner of a Packt book, we have a number of things to help you to get the most from your purchase.

Downloading the example code

You can download the example code files from your account at http://www.packtpub.com for all the Packt Publishing books you have purchased. If you purchased this book elsewhere, you can visit http://www.packtpub.com/support and register to have the files e-mailed directly to you.

Errata

Although we have taken every care to ensure the accuracy of our content, mistakes do happen. If you find a mistake in one of our books—maybe a mistake in the text or the code—we would be grateful if you could report this to us. By doing so, you can save other readers from frustration and help us improve subsequent versions of this book. If you find any errata, please report them by visiting http://www.packtpub. com/submit-errata, selecting your book, clicking on the **Errata Submission Form** link, and entering the details of your errata. Once your errata are verified, your submission will be accepted and the errata will be uploaded to our website or added to any list of existing errata under the Errata section of that title.

To view the previously submitted errata, go to https://www.packtpub.com/books/ content/support and enter the name of the book in the search field. The required information will appear under the **Errata** section.

Piracy

Piracy of copyrighted material on the Internet is an ongoing problem across all media. At Packt, we take the protection of our copyright and licenses very seriously. If you come across any illegal copies of our works in any form on the Internet, please provide us with the location address or website name immediately so that we can pursue a remedy.

Please contact us at copyright@packtpub.com with a link to the suspected pirated material.

We appreciate your help in protecting our authors and our ability to bring you valuable content.

Questions

If you have a problem with any aspect of this book, you can contact us at questions@packtpub.com, and we will do our best to address the problem.

1
Getting Started with High Availability

We live in a fast-paced world and, with all the technology surrounding us, we take it for granted most of the time. When we set the alarm clock in the evening before falling asleep, we never give much thought whether the alarm will actually work in the morning or not; and when we turn the ignition key to drive off to work, we never stop to think whether the car will fail to start or not. On a normal day, there is hardly any chance of anything like this happening to us, so we can calmly go to sleep in the evening. The same applies to visiting our favorite website first thing in the morning. We are, in fact, more likely to expect that the car will not start or the bus will be late than that we will not be able to log in to our Facebook or Gmail account. No wonder, these sites are is always online and ready to serve information whenever we request it.

Have you ever asked yourself, "How can this be?" We all know we cannot trust technology implicitly. Sooner or later, it can and it will fail. With such complex systems and technologies surrounding us, we are actually not aware how many systems are required to run flawlessly so that we can read our e-mails and check our Facebook walls. How did we become so sure that these complex systems will always provide what we require?

The answer to the question is high availability. Highly available systems are what made us all blind, in the belief that services are always there and on and failure is not an option. As the title of this book suggests, the objective is to familiarize you with how to achieve high availability, focusing on an actual, practical example of a three-node cluster configuration on CentOS Linux version 6 and 7. A three-node cluster is chosen because the number of cluster nodes plays a key role in the cluster configuration process, which will be explained in more detail later in the book. You will become familiar with two different software solutions available for achieving high availability on CentOS Linux.

In the first chapter, you will learn about high availability in general. It will start by laying the foundation and explaining what high availability is, also describing what system design approaches must be followed to make an IT system highly available. We will explain the meaning of computer clusters, why we need them, and the possible computer cluster configurations.

The emphasis of this book is on the following topics:

- A practical, hands-on user guide
- Cluster software installation and configuration
- Cluster resource configuration and management
- Cluster node management
- Cluster failover testing

What is high availability?

The general meaning of the word "availability" is a characteristic of a resource — either a person or an object that can be accessed or used. Resource availability can be measured, and therefore, a ratio of the time a resource is accessible or usable to the time the resource is inaccessible or unusable can be calculated. Adding an adjective "high" to the word "availability" suggests that the resource should be accessible and usable most of the time during a given time interval. The term "high availability" is commonly used in information technology and it describes IT systems with a high level of availability.

High availability in IT refers to a system that is continuously operational and available for the delivery of services it provides for end users. The key point when talking about IT systems is the availability to deliver services to end users, since a system can be up-and-running from the IT administrator's perspective but can fail to provide services for end users, which makes it useless. There are a number of factors that can lead to service downtime, mainly because there are so many different layers that must work together to provide service availability.

An IT system usually consists of many different components. All of these components must be continuously available for a desirable length of time. It is needless to say that it is very important for these highly available systems to be properly designed, well thought through, and thoroughly tested with the goal of eliminating any possibility of potential failure. That being said, high availability is a system design approach, and a service implementation in a way, to provide the highest achievable level of performance and availability by eliminating all system-wide single points of failure.

Not every system can be marked highly available. It is common practice in IT to measure and calculate the availability of a system. Monitoring tools such as **Nagios**, **Zenoss**, or **Zabbix** can be used to provide reports on system availability and also alerts in the case of system unavailability. The measurements taken must reflect the actual availability of the system to the end user. By measuring and calculating the availability of a system, we can split them into systems that are classified as highly available and systems that are not. System availability is commonly expressed as a percentage of system uptime in a given year.

System design

IT systems that offer high availability of services must follow a specific system design approach by which they can provide the most available continuous operation. The fundamental rule of a high-availability system design approach is to avoid single points of failure. A single point of failure is a component of a system that could lead to system and service downtime if it fails. The design should avoid single points of failure, which makes the system more robust and automatically increases system and service availability.

A complex IT system providing application services can have a large number of single points of failure at different levels, but how can we eliminate all of them? The solution is redundancy. Redundancy means duplication of the system's critical components. Duplication of devices allows continuous system operation even if one of the duplicated devices fails. There are two types of redundancy: passive and active. Passive redundancy means using two or more devices while only one of them provides its service at certain point in time. The other devices wait to take over in the case of an unrecoverable failure of the operating device. Active redundancy means using two or more devices, all providing their service at all times. Even if one of the devices fails, other devices are continuously providing the service.

Let me try to explain single points of failure and redundancy with a practical example. Let's say you are hosting a simple website on your personal home computer. The computer is located at your home, hidden in your storage closet. It is happily providing a website service for end users. It is always on and users can access the website any time of the day. If you and I were ignorant, we could say that you are running a perfect solution with a perfect system design, especially since you are saving a fair amount of money, not paying for expensive hosting solutions at your local hosting service. But stop to think for a second and try to count the single points of failure in the system's design. Running a website on a personal computer that is not a dedicated server machine has a number of single points of failure to begin with. Personal computers are not designed to run continuously, mostly due to the fact that the hardware components of a personal computer are not duplicated and the redundancy requirements for high availability are not met.

If the hard drive on your personal computer fails, the system will crash and the website will experience serious downtime. The same goes for the computer's power supply. Unexpected failure of any of these components will bring the website down for anything ranging from an hour to days. The period of the downtime depends on the availability of the replacement component and the backup solution implemented. Another major issue with the system design in the provided example is the Internet Service Provider and the connection to the World Wide Web. Your personal computer is relying only on a single source to provide its Internet service and connection. If the Internet Service Provider, for some reason, suddenly experiences huge network problems and your Internet service goes down, the website will also experience serious downtime and you will be losing visitors—and possibly money—with every minute the website is unreachable. Again, the same goes for the electricity supply. You need to provide redundant components in every possible aspect, not just hardware. Redundancy must be provided at all layers, including the networking layer, power supply layer, and also the yet unmentioned application layer.

Nowadays the majority of modern server systems eliminate hardware single points of failure by duplicating hardware components, but this solution still falls short of eliminating single points of failure in applications, which is one of the main reasons for using computer cluster implementation. Application-layer redundancy is achieved with computer clusters. A computer cluster is a group of computers running cluster software that enables continuous two-way communication, also called a **heartbeat**, between cluster members. A heartbeat provides cluster members with information on the exact status of any cluster member at any given time. Practically, this means that any member of the cluster knows the exact number of the members in the cluster it is joined to and also knows which cluster members are active or online, in maintenance mode, offline, and many more aspects.

Computer clusters

A computer cluster is a group of computers joined to work together in order to provide high availability of some services. The services are usually built with a number of applications operating in the so-called application layer. As shown in the example from the previous section, single points of failure are spread across all layers of a system design, and the application layer is one of the critical layers. It is usual for an application to encounter an error, or bug, and stop responding or crash. Such a situation will lead to service downtime and probably financial loss as well, so it is necessary to provide redundancy on the application layer also. This is the reason we need to implement a computer cluster solution into our high-availability system design.

A computer cluster consists of two or more computers. The computers are connected to the local area network. The maximum number of computers in a computer cluster is limited by the cluster software solution implemented but, in general, common cluster solutions support at least 16 cluster members. It is good practice for the cluster members to have the same hardware and specifications, which means that the cluster computers consist of components from the same manufacturer and likely have the same resource specifications.

There are two common types of computer clusters:

- Load balancing computer clusters
- High-availability computer clusters

Load balancing computer clusters are used to provide better and higher performance of services, and are typically used in science for complex scientific measurements and calculations. Interestingly, the same clusters are also used for websites and web servers facing extremely high load, which helps improve the overall response of the website with load distribution to different cluster nodes.

High-availability computer clusters strive to minimize the downtime of the service provided and not so much to improve the overall performance of the service. The focus of this book is on high-availability clusters. There are many different cluster configurations, mainly depending on the number of cluster members and also on the level of availability you want to achieve.

Some of the different cluster configurations are as follows:

- **Active/Active**: The Active/Active cluster configuration can be used with two or more cluster members. The service provided by the cluster is simultaneously active on all cluster nodes at any given time. The traffic can be passed to any of the existing cluster nodes if a suitable load balancing solution has been implemented. If no load balancing solution has been implemented, the Active/Active configuration can be used to reduce the time it takes to fail over applications and services from the failed cluster node.

- **Active/Passive**: The Active/Passive cluster configuration can be used with two or more cluster members. At a given time, the service is provided only by the current master cluster node. If the master node fails, automatic reconfiguration of the cluster is triggered and the traffic is switched to one of the operational cluster nodes.

- **N + 1**: The N over 1 cluster configuration can be used with two or more cluster members. If only two cluster members are available, the configuration degenerates to the Active/Passive configuration. The N over 1 configuration implies the presence of N cluster members in an active/active configuration with one cluster member in backup or hot standby. The standby cluster member is ready to take over any of the failed cluster node responsibilities at any given time.

- **N + M**: The N over M cluster configuration can only be used with more than two cluster members. This configuration is an upgrade of the N over 1 cluster configuration where N cluster members are in Active/Active state and M cluster members are in backup or hot standby mode. This is often used in situations where active cluster members manage many services and two or more backup cluster members are required to fulfill the cluster failover requirements.

- **N-to-1**: The N-to-1 cluster configuration is similar to the N over 1 configuration and can be used with two or more cluster members. If there are only two cluster nodes, this configuration degenerates to Active/Passive. In the N-to-1 configuration, the backup or hot standby cluster member becomes temporarily active for the time period of failed cluster node recovery. When the failed cluster node is recovered, services are failed over to the original cluster node.

- **N-to-N**: The N-to-N cluster configuration is similar to the N over M configuration and can be used with more than two cluster nodes. This configuration is an upgrade of the N-to-1 configuration and is used in situations where the need for extra redundancy is required on all active nodes.

The objective of a high-availability computer cluster is to provide uninterrupted and continuous availability of the service provided by the applications running in the cluster. There are many applications available that provide all sorts of services, but not every application can be managed and configured to work in a cluster. You need to make sure that the applications you choose to run in your computer cluster are easy to start, stop, and monitor. In this way, the cluster software can make instant application status checks, starts, and stops.

A computer cluster cannot exist without a shared storage solution. It is quite clear that a cluster is useless if the cluster members have access only to their local storage and data. The cluster members must have access to some kind of shared storage solution that ensures that all cluster members are able to access the same data. Cluster member access to the same storage provides consistency throughout the computer cluster. There are many shared storage solutions available, of which the following are the most commonly used in computer clusters today:

- **Storage Area Network (SAN)**: This is a type of block-level data storage. It provides high-speed data transfers and **Redundant Array of Inexpensive Disks (RAID)** disk redundancy. The most commonly used SAN solutions are big storage racks of disk arrays with hundreds of disks and terabytes of disk space. These storage racks are connected to computers via optical fibers to achieve the highest possible performance. Computers can see the storage as locally attached storage devices and are free to create the desired file system on these devices.

- **Network-attached Storage (NAS)**: This is a type of file-level data storage. With an NAS solution, the file system is predefined and forced on the client computers. NAS also provides RAID disk redundancy and the capability to expand to hundreds of disks and terabytes of disk space. As the name suggests, NAS storage is connected to computers through the network and provides access to data using file-sharing protocols such as **Network File System (NFS)**, **Server Message Block (SMB)**, and **Apple Filling Protocol (AFP)**. Computers see NAS storage as network drives that they can map locally.

- **Distributed Replicated Block Device (DRBD)**: This is probably the least expensive and most interesting solution. DRBD is a network-based mirrored disk redundancy. It is installed and configured on computers as a service and those computers can use their existing local storage to mirror and replicate data through the network. DRBD is a software solution that runs on the Linux platform, and was released in July 2007. It was quickly merged with the Linux kernel by 2009. It is probably the simplest and cheapest to implement into any system design as long as it is Linux-based.

High-availability solutions

Nowadays, there are many different high-availability solutions you can choose from. Some of them are implemented on completely different layers and offer different levels of high availability. Even though some of these solutions are fairly easy to implement and provide a significantly high level of availability, they cannot compete with complete high-availability solutions and fall short compared to them.

Virtualization is the first step to be mention. Virtualization has taken large steps forward in the last decade, and probably everyone is using it. It became really popular very quickly, mostly due to the fact that it significantly lowers the cost of server maintenance, boosts the server life cycle, and facilitates management of the servers. Almost every virtualization solution also provides an integrated high-availability option that allows virtualization hosts to be joined with virtualization clusters.

The solution instantly provides high availability of virtual machines running on top of it. Therefore, the virtualization high-availability solution is provided on the lower virtualization layer. However, this kind of high availability might still fall short in certain key points. It only manages to eliminate the hardware single points of failure. It does not implement high availability of the applications and services that the virtual machines are running.

Databases are also one of the components of IT infrastructure with built-in high-availability solutions. Database servers are known to provide mission-critical services, mostly due to the huge amount of important data they usually store. This is why common database server software products offer high-availability features bundled with the database server software. This means that it is possible to implement database high availability at the database application layer. Database server high availability can provide the top application layer with high availability, which does not cover all angles required for a complete high-availability solution.

A complete high-availability solution is considered to be a solution that is implemented at the operating system level and includes the application layer, of course backed up by hardware, power supply, and network connection redundancy. This kind of high-availability solution is resistant to hardware and application failures and allows you to achieve the highest possible availability of the service.

Summary

In this chapter, you got a general idea of what high availability is. You learned how high availability is achieved and what system design approach must be followed to get it right. Then you became familiar with computer clusters and cluster configurations, while also exploring the most commonly used types of shared storage solutions. In the following chapters, you will get to know cluster software layers and their tasks in greater detail.

2
Meet the Cluster Stack on CentOS

The previous chapter, familiarized you with high availability and computer clusters were introduced. You learned that the key components of clusters are computers as cluster members and they run computer cluster software. In this chapter, you will learn how computer clusters work. You will get to know the software that builds a computer cluster, allowing it to function as expected, and the tasks each cluster software component has.

Computers forming a computer cluster must be running a piece of cluster software, which is a bundle of many components. Each of these components has a different task and all of these components work together to satisfy all the cluster requirements and provide the features a computer cluster must implement.

Cluster stack is a phrase used to describe the cluster software used to form a computer cluster. A cluster stack is a software stack and it includes all of the necessary software for normal operation of a cluster. The software included in the cluster stack is divided with respect to its primary tasks. When deciding which cluster software to use, you must focus on the cluster software's reliability, simplicity, features, and also the course of development. There are many different solutions to setting up and configuring a computer cluster, as it can run on different platforms and different operating systems. In this chapter, we will focus on explaining the details of a cluster stack and cluster stack layers, and you will also become familiar with CentOS Linux cluster stack solutions.

Cluster stack software

A computer cluster is a group of computers working together as one unit. A computer cluster can, in many ways, be viewed as a single system, even though it is built from many computers. All cluster members are closely connected, each one of them being prepared to take any actions needed at any time. This sounds simple but, actually, it requires complex software products and solutions for a computer cluster to operate in this way. A cluster software stack makes sure that all the magic happens. It introduces a bundle of combined software products to form a complete high-availability computer cluster solution. It is a software stack and its goal is to provide a highly available cluster service.

Generally speaking, the cluster software stack must provide two significant features:

- **Cluster communication**: This is located at the bottom layer of the cluster stack due to its close relation to the transport layer. Communication between cluster members is only possible via the transport layer and one of the well-known protocols. It depends on the choice of cluster communication software as to which transport layer protocols the communication supports. The most commonly used protocols for cluster communication are multicast or broadcast **TCP/IP** and **UDP/IP**. Multicast is a one-to-many or many-to-many group communication process where information can be addressed to a group of destination computers simultaneously, whereas broadcast is one-to-many-specific. One-to-many or many-to-many group communication is usually preferred for cluster communication because it reduces the time for cluster communication in general.

- **Cluster resource management**: This is the top layer of the cluster stack due to its connection to operating system applications. Cluster resource management starts, stops, and manages applications in the cluster in general. It relies on the cluster communication layer to get the information it requires about cluster members and their status, and takes cluster resource actions based on that. Cluster communication software and cluster resource management software work together synchronously.

The following diagram represents the communication process among four different service layers. It shows how the cluster stack software fits between the service layers:

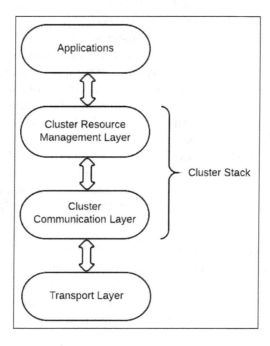

When you are building a computer cluster, you usually plan the cluster to run for years to come. This implies that the computer cluster software stack must maintain active development at least for the desired cluster implementation time. It is common sense that you use software that is actively maintained and developed while cluster communication layer provides you with security patches, bug fixes, and enhancement updates.

Let's explore the cluster communication layer and cluster resource management in detail.

The cluster communication layer

The cluster communication layer is the bottom layer of the cluster software stack and provides continuous communication between all the computer cluster nodes. Continuous communication between the cluster members is required for normal cluster operation. It is a priority for cluster members to get all of the information required about the current computer cluster configuration and status at any time. The cluster members must always know the exact number of the cluster nodes currently forming the computer cluster, and must also be notified immediately if a cluster member joins or leaves the computer cluster. Successful cluster communication can be achieved only when all the cluster members are connected to each other and able to communicate. This is why you must carefully decide the sort of cluster connection the members will use to communicate to each other. The types of supported cluster connection are defined by the cluster communication software. The most common types of cluster communication are TCP/IP, UDP/IP Serial connection, **InfiniBand**, and so on.

- The most widely used is the TCP/IP or UDP/IP connection, depending on the network environment you are implementing the solution in. TCP is connection-oriented and highly reliable, while UDP is connectionless, faster, and more efficient in a noncongested network environment. The cluster communication layer provides the following services to ensure normal cluster operation:
- The cluster messaging and membership service
- Quorum

The cluster messaging and membership service

A special protocol called **Totem Single-ring Ordering and Membership (TOTEM)** was developed to provide cluster group communication. TOTEM provides cluster messaging and membership services. The cluster messaging service is the communication process among cluster members. This communication process is called a **heartbeat** and the formation cluster members adopt is called a **ring**. Each cluster member constantly sends heartbeats to other cluster members. With heartbeats, cluster members let each other know that they are operational. After a series of heartbeats from a specific cluster member is lost or undelivered, the membership service steps in and lets other cluster members know that a specific cluster member is down and a cluster reconfiguration is required. When the operational cluster members reach Quorum, the membership service performs a cluster reconfiguration. Once the cluster reconfiguration completes, the process of cluster messaging is restored to normal.

The TOTEM protocol provides an ordered message delivery with low overhead, high throughput, and low latency. TOTEM uses the broadcast method to send messages to all recipients simultaneously. This method is very similar to the multicast method mentioned before. The only difference between the two is that broadcast can be used only as a one-to-many group communication and multicast also supports many-to-many communication. TOTEM delivers all messages in an agreed order, which guarantees message consistency throughout the cluster. This means that, when a cluster member sends a communication message to other cluster members, the member can be sure that it has already delivered all prior messages it had to deliver to other members. This kind of operation is not easy to maintain, especially in an environment subject to failures. To solve this problem, the TOTEM protocol introduces a special token, passed among the cluster members. Only the cluster member that possesses this token can broadcast messages to other cluster members. Each cluster member has an incoming message buffer, where it stores the received messages. The message headers store a unique sequence number, that is derived from the token. Therefore, the order of the messages is fixed with the sequence number. Even with the message passing token, different cluster members may get the information as a result of any change in cluster configuration at different times. Cluster members may have received some additional messages still stored in the buffer, making them inconsistent with the other cluster members. To mitigate this problem, an additional concept (virtual synchrony) was introduced, ensuring that cluster members deliver messages consistently, even in the event of cluster node failure. The virtual synchrony concept was extended to allow continued operation with a so-called temporary transitional cluster configuration with reduced membership in case of cluster member failures.

In the following diagram, you can see the process of four-node cluster communication via the TOTEM protocol. Cluster node **A** is currently in possession of the token and is broadcasting messages to other cluster members through the local network:

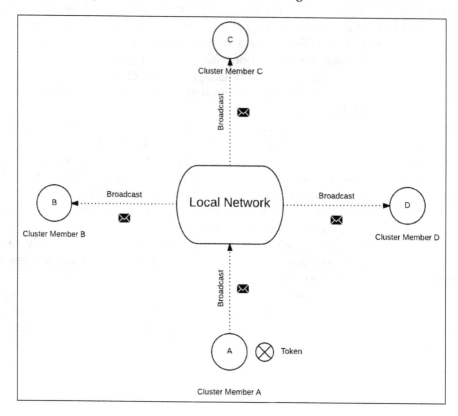

The TOTEM protocol is optimized for high messaging performance but does not excel in cluster member failure scenarios. An additional extension to the TOTEM protocol was introduced to address the issue of membership. It is called the **membership protocol**. The membership protocol was designed to address the issue of cluster member failure, network communication failure, or the loss of the message passing token. The membership protocol detects cluster member failures and rebuilds the cluster configuration, leaving out failed cluster members. The primary task of the membership protocol is to achieve consensus between cluster members. This means that all the cluster members agree on the change in the cluster configuration and also successfully install a new cluster configuration within an agreed period of time. A new passing token is also generated. All of these processes enable the TOTEM protocol to resume normal operation of the cluster messaging system after a cluster failure.

Quorum

Another very important process managed by the cluster communication layer is called **Quorum**. Quorum is the minimum number of cluster member votes required to perform a cluster operation. When failure of a cluster member occurs, an immediate cluster reconfiguration is required. On failure, the number of operational cluster members changes, and the remaining cluster members must propose a cluster reconfiguration. The operational cluster members must make a decision on the cluster node the failed services will be recovered at. This decision is not up an individual cluster member; it has to be voted and agreed upon. This is where the quorum process comes into play. Based on the current cluster status, quorum must be reached among the cluster members and the final decision must be accepted. The cluster member votes are required to achieve a majority in order to reach quorum, and each cluster member only has one vote. Some cluster communication software solutions support an additional quorum disk that counts as an additional so-called tie-breaker vote. The quorum disk is very useful and also required in an even-node cluster configuration. In the first chapter, we mentioned that building a cluster with an even number of cluster nodes is more convenient. This is mostly due to quorum voting. In a two-node cluster, only two votes are available from the cluster nodes, which means that, in the event of a cluster failure, the operational cluster node does not have quorum majority and can't make decisions. The quorum disk is a shared storage disk to which all the cluster members have access. All the cluster members use the quorum disk for heartbeat communication and store cluster configuration data in it. Based on the activity on the quorum disk, cluster members can run their cluster communication via the quorum disk, and the quorum disk can also count as a vote in the quorum process. The quorum disk is a must in an even-node cluster configuration.

Another interesting condition we must mention is a **split brain**. Split brain is a condition in the cluster where the cluster is split into two sides, each side thinking that the other side is dead or inactive. In this situation, each side proceeds to take over the resources as if the other side no longer exists. To prevent such scenarios, an additional mechanism called **fencing** is used. Before any of the split sides of the cluster takes over the resources, the fencing mechanism fences the other side by issuing a configured action of reboot or power-off on the cluster nodes, thus making sure that the cluster nodes on the other side are really dead. Once successful fencing is confirmed, the operational side can safely start the resources without any data corruption or disruption. We will explain fencing in more detail in later chapters.

The cluster resource management layer

The cluster resource management layer is the top layer of the cluster stack. It makes sure that the services your cluster provides are up-and-running at all times.

The features of the cluster resource management layer are as follows:

- Starting cluster resources
- Stopping cluster resources
- Monitoring cluster resources
- Migrating cluster resources
- Grouping cluster resources
- Location constraints

The main objective of the cluster resource management layer is to relocate cluster resources and services to operational cluster members when there is a failure in the cluster. In order for the cluster resource management layer to manage cluster services, it must be able to access the applications providing the cluster service. The services and applications the cluster resource manager provides are called **cluster resources**. These resources can be anything such as an IP address, web server, database server, or any other application available on the operating system. The cluster resource manager is required to manage and, more importantly, monitor the cluster resources. This is achievable through specific cluster resource agents provided by the cluster resource manager or also through so-called Linux `init` scripts — start and stop scripts provided by the applications.

The cluster resource manager provides high availability of cluster services by detecting and recovering cluster service failure from the cluster nodes and cluster resource failures. This is done with the help of, and information from, the bottom cluster communication layer. The cluster communication layer continuously communicates with the cluster resource management layer, exchanging information about the status of each cluster member. When a cluster member failure is detected, a notification is immediately sent to the cluster resource manager and the required actions are taken. The cluster resource manager starts the cluster service reconfiguration process and relocates the cluster resources to one of the remaining nodes, as agreed in the quorum process.

The full set of features differentiates among the pieces of cluster resource manager software used but, in general, the cluster resource manager also provides a resource grouping feature. This feature allows you to group resources together in a cluster service, ensuring they are run together on the same cluster node. Additionally, you can configure a start-and-stop order of the grouped resources and also the cluster node location preference. An important task to mention is fencing. There are two types of fencing: resource-level fencing and node-level fencing. Resource-level fencing is the way the cluster disables a specific or problematic node to access a specific resource. This is usually used on shared storage resources, where a problematic node is denied access to certain shared storage. More commonly used is node-level fencing. Node-level fencing is a way to make sure a node does not run any resources at all. This is usually the case on some obscure cluster node failures and unresponsiveness or network failures. The cluster is not aware of the exact cause of node unresponsiveness, but it needs to make sure the problematic cluster node is generally banned from the computer cluster. Node fencing is also called **STONITH**, which stands for **Shoot The Other Node In The Head**. Node fencing can be achieved in many ways using different sorts of fencing devices. Which fencing devices are supported depends on the cluster resource manager software. The additional features of STONITH will be explained in more detail in the following chapters, with practical examples of cluster resource manager configuration.

As you can see, the cluster resource manager is just as complex as the cluster communication layer software, but provides a lot more cluster tasks. The following is an example of a cluster environment. This is just an example of a small clustered web service; the cluster can provide a number of other services.

A theoretical cluster service example

In order to make it easy for you to understand the cluster service, you will be presented with a theoretical example of a two-node active/passive computer cluster providing a website cluster service. The active/passive cluster configuration only provides operational cluster services on the master cluster member at a given time, while the secondary cluster member waits on standby to take over if there is a master node failure. If the currently active cluster member fails, the cluster resources will be relocated and recovered on the operational secondary cluster member.

The following resources are required to run a simple website:

- IP address — web server
- Database server
- Shared storage solution

All the listed resources must be installed and configured on the cluster node operating system and also added to the cluster resource manager configuration. In this way, the cluster resource manager is able to manage the resources and provide failover capabilities. The resources must follow a specific start-and-stop order, allowing the website to be accessible to end users. The start-and-stop order of cluster resources is configurable through the cluster resource manager.

The following start order of the resources should apply:

1. IP address.
2. Database server.
3. Web server.
4. Here is the stop order of the resources to be applied:
5. Web server.
6. Database server.
7. IP address.

Let's look at the start order of the cluster resources a bit more closely:

- **IP address**: The IP address resource should always be the first cluster resource to start. This is due to the fact that network-oriented applications and services bind to the configured IP address on startup. If the IP address is not available, the service startup will fail.

- **Database server**: Next in order is the database server. This provides crucial website data. If the database server is not accessible on web server startup, the website will miss data that is vital for normal operation.

- **Web server**: The last to start is the web server. The web server acts as the end user contact point; therefore, it must not start until you are absolutely sure the website will provide what the service end users require.

In the following diagram, you can see the graphical presentation of the cluster provided in the example. At the bottom are the cluster nodes, followed by the cluster stack software and the shared storage. At the top are the cluster resources, currently running on the active cluster. In the case of active cluster node failure, the direction of cluster resource failover is marked.

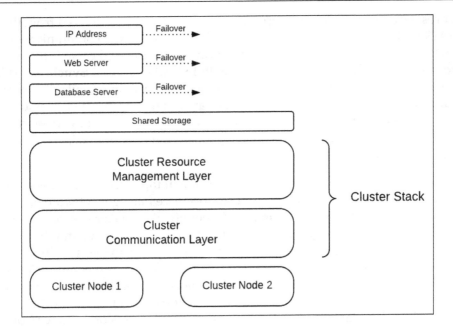

Cluster stack on CentOS Linux

There are endless possibilities and platforms a computer cluster can be installed and configured on and, therefore, also different software building the cluster stack. Since the objectives of this book are to familiarize you with the high-availability cluster running on CentOS Linux, I will present you with the cluster stack software to be used to install and configure a highly available computer cluster on CentOS Linux.

CentOS is a **Community Enterprise Operating System**. It is a Linux distribution that provides a free enterprise platform. The functionalities of CentOS are compatible with its commercial upstream source: **Red Hat Enterprise Linux (RHEL)**. The current major CentOS version is 7 and was released on July 7, 2014. It offers many changes compared to its predecessor, CentOS version 6. Probably due to this and the fact that CentOS 6 maintenance updates will be supported until November 30, 2020, the majority of CentOS Linux servers still run CentOS version 6. This is the reason this book covers cluster installation and configuration on CentOS version 6 and 7. I must point out that the cluster stack software used in the upcoming practical examples of the book, and installed and configured on CentOS version 6, is no longer available on CentOS 7. Both the cluster solutions presented in the following chapters will provide full, highly available computer cluster solutions for CentOS 6 and CentOS 7. The only difference between the two versions is the cluster resource manager software used. This means that both solutions will use the same cluster communication software, called **Corosync**.

The Corosync cluster engine is an open source project that was derived from the **OpenAIS** project and was announced in July 2008. It is a group communication system that provides all the cluster communication features and capabilities. It provides a service of the TOTEM protocol with **Extended Virtual Synchrony** (**EVS**) for messaging and membership. It is also shipped with a simple availability manager that can restart the application process in the case of failure. Corosync provides a Quorum system, notifying the cluster resource manager of the voting process as required. Corosync is being actively developed and the Corosync 2.3.4 Needle was released at the end of 2014.

Since cluster resource manager software must run on top of Corosync, this is where the road splits into two. There are two cluster resource manager software options to use—either **RGManager** or **Pacemaker**. Generally, Pacemaker has more features than RGManager. RGManager development is known to be slower and therefore less mutable, which can also be a good thing when it comes to the stability of the software. RGManager also requires the **CMAN** software as the middle layer between it and Corosync. CMAN is the communication layer between Corosync and RGManager, also providing some additional functionality. It is an interesting fact that the official Red Hat Cluster software suite in RHEL 6 version includes Corosync, CMAN, and RGManager; in RHEL 7, however, this was changed to Corosync and Pacemaker. Since CentOS is closely related to RHEL, CMAN and RGManager are no longer available in CentOS version 7. If you are planning a new implementation and installation of the computer cluster, I recommend using CentOS version 7 with the Corosync and Pacemaker cluster stack, which is the ultimate solution. However, you may want to go with Corosync, CMAN, and RGManager on CentOS 6, so a practical example of this configuration will also be provided for you.

Preparing for cluster stack software installation

The first step towards building your highly available computer cluster is the operating system installation. We will not cover the details of installing CentOS Linux on the server machines. I can only mention that it is always good practice to install the minimum number of packages required. This is the beauty of using the Linux operating system in general, and also CentOS Linux specifically. CentOS has an option for minimal installation, which actually installs only the basic required packages for normal functioning of the operating system. This is an advantage because the more packages are used, the higher the possibility that one of the packages will go berserk and cause trouble at the operating system level. It is also an advantage for patching the systems, since there are fewer packages to patch.

All the dependencies and required packages will be installed while installing the cluster stack software of your choice. Note that you can always install additional packages if you require them.

Once the operating system is installed and running, additional requirements must be met for normal operation. Operational cluster node communication is a crucial part of the cluster operation, and you need to make sure that cluster-wide cluster node communication is guaranteed. Each of the cluster nodes must be assigned a reserved static IP address, and all cluster nodes must be able to communicate with each other. The cluster nodes must be configured to communicate via an IP address and also the **Fully Qualified Domain Name** (**FQDN**) domain names, which requires proper configuration of DNS servers. It is also highly recommended to configure NTP date and time synchronization for all the cluster nodes. In this way, you can be sure that all the cluster members are synchronized to the same NTP servers and are therefore sharing the same date and time settings. It is known to be good practice that the DNS and NTP servers are in the same local network area as the cluster nodes, thus reducing the possibility of network failure causing problems in the DNS resolution or NTP synchronization. To simplify and shorten command-line statements, you can also reduce the FQDN names of the cluster nodes to shorter descriptive names. This can help in situations where you must review lots of lines of logging information, which is more readable with shorter node names. **Secure Shell** (**SSH**) is also a convenient way of moving the configuration or other files around the cluster nodes and also running remote commands on them. SSH provides key authentication and **Secure Copy** (**SCP**) commands for file transfer. In your cluster environment, SSH keys should be replicated, allowing passwordless (and quicker and more efficient) file transfer.

Summary

In this chapter, you became familiar with cluster stacks and cluster stack layers. Each cluster stack layer was explained in detail by elaborating on the tasks it must provide and how to provide them. You also learned about the cluster software stack solutions that will be presented in practical examples in the following chapters of this book, and the necessary preparations and recommendations before installing the cluster software stack. In the next chapter, you will prepare the operating system to run the cluster stack software. You will follow step-by-step instructions on how to install and configure operating system requirements and cluster communication software.

3
Cluster Stack Software on CentOS 6

If you've decided to install cluster stack software on CentOS version 6, you will be installing and configuring Corosync with the CMAN cluster messaging layer and the RGManager cluster resource manager. Corosync with the CMAN cluster messaging layer and the RGManager cluster resource manager cluster stack software are part of the official Red Hat Enterprise Linux version 6 cluster suite; due to CentOS's close relationship with RHEL, using RGManager on CentOS version 6 is the way to go.

With the release of Red Hat Enterprise Linux version 7, the official Red Hat cluster suite changed. The Red Hat 7 cluster suite includes Corosync as the cluster messaging layer software and Pacemaker as the cluster resource management layer software. If your preferred choice is CentOS version 7 and the Pacemaker cluster resource manager, jump to *Chapter 9, Cluster Stack Software on CentOS 7*. That chapter (and the chapters that follow it) covers the installation and configuration of Corosync and Pacemaker on CentOS version 7.

Cluster infrastructure

In forthcoming chapters, you will be presented with a practical example of cluster installation and configuration. The three-node cluster used in the example will be running in a virtualized environment. All cluster node virtual machines run on a CentOS version 6 64-bit minimal installation. **SELinux** and **IPTables** are enabled and run on all cluster nodes. All the cluster nodes have the same resource specifications, as follows:

- One CPU core
- 768 MB RAM

- One 10 GB disk
- One 1 GB disk
- Two network adapters

The cluster node's fully qualified domain names are as follows:

- node-1.geekpeek.net (short name: node-1)
- node-2.geekpeek.net (short name: node-2)
- node-3.geekpeek.net (short name: node-3)

Due to the limitations of my virtualized environment, the network IP addresses of both cluster node network interfaces are in the same network subnet: `192.168.88.0/24`.

The assigned static cluster node IP addresses are as follows:

- `192.168.88.10`, `192.168.88.11`: node-1.geekpeek.net
- `192.168.88.20`, `192.168.88.21`: node-2.geekpeek.net
- `192.168.88.30`, `192.168.88.31`: node-3.geekpeek.net

It is preferred to have a separate network subnet for cluster communication and for all other cases of traffic. For production environments, each cluster node should have at least two network interfaces. The cluster node's messaging traffic should be separated from all other instances of traffic, and usually divided with a different network subnet configuration.

Cluster operating system preparation

I assume your cluster nodes are all set up; power, network and other cables are connected; the operating system is installed; and disks are partitioned the way you want them. Before you can start with the installation and configuration of the cluster stack software, you must carefully follow these steps:

1. **Network configuration**: You must configure a static IP address for all available network interfaces on all cluster nodes. You can do this by editing the `/etc/sysconfig/network-scripts/ifcfg-ethX` files. You must also disable the Network Manager network interface control. In the following screenshot, you can see the network interface configuration for the **node-1** cluster node:

```
                           root@node-1:~                              x

 File  Edit  View  Search  Terminal  Help
[root@node-1 ~]# cat /etc/sysconfig/network-scripts/ifcfg-eth0
DEVICE=eth0
HWADDR=08:00:27:A6:97:AB
UUID=451aace0-4d02-4a60-bc31-4fb8d2705481
TYPE=Ethernet
ONBOOT=yes
NM_CONTROLLED=no
BOOTPROTO=none
IPADDR=192.168.88.10
NETMASK=255.255.255.0
GATEWAY=192.168.88.1
[root@node-1 ~]# cat /etc/sysconfig/network-scripts/ifcfg-eth1
DEVICE=eth1
HWADDR=08:00:27:88:48:19
UUID=6dfd1ad2-395c-4c0b-9576-73d097acfdd7
TYPE=Ethernet
ONBOOT=yes
NM_CONTROLLED=no
BOOTPROTO=none
IPADDR=192.168.88.11
NETMASK=255.255.255.0
GATEWAY=192.168.88.1
[root@node-1 ~]#
```

Change the NM_CONTROLLED line to no. This specifies that the Network Manager service cannot control the network interface.

Change the BOOTPROTO line to none. This specifies that no boot protocol is used for this interface, since this interface has a static IP address assigned to it.

Add the IPADDR, NETMASK, and GATEWAY lines according to your environment and networking configuration. To complete the networking part, you must restart the networking service. In the following screenshot, you can see the network restart on the **node-1** cluster node:

```
                           root@node-1:~                              x

 File  Edit  View  Search  Terminal  Help
[root@node-1 ~]# service network restart
Shutting down interface eth0:                            [  OK  ]
Shutting down interface eth1:                            [  OK  ]
Shutting down loopback interface:                        [  OK  ]
Bringing up loopback interface:                          [  OK  ]
Bringing up interface eth0:  Determining if ip address 192.168.88.10
is already in use for device eth0...
                                                         [  OK  ]
Bringing up interface eth1:  Determining if ip address 192.168.88.11
is already in use for device eth1...
                                                         [  OK  ]
[root@node-1 ~]#
```

Note that you must reconfigure all network interfaces and restart networking service on all cluster nodes.

2. **NTP configuration**: You must install and start the NTP time synchronization service to maintain consistent time throughout the cluster:

```
[root@node-1 ~]# yum install ntp -y
```

In this screenshot, you can see the command used to install the NTP time synchronization service:

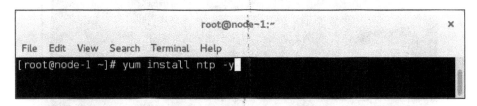

By default, NTP installation time is synchronized with official CentOS NTP servers. If you want to change this, edit the NTP configuration file at `/etc/ntp.conf`.

You must start the NTP service and make sure it starts at boot. In the following screenshot, you can see the commands used:

```
[root@node-1 ~]# service ntpd start
[root@node-1 ~]# chkconfig ntpd on
```

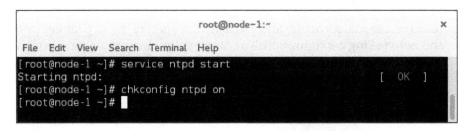

 You must install and start the NTP service on all cluster nodes, and do not forget to make it start at boot.

3. **DNS configuration**: You must configure the domain name servers, fully qualified domain names, and the hosts file. The domain name service is provided by the DNS servers, which are configured in the /etc/resolv. conf file. It is recommended you configure at least two DNS servers; you can add more if you like. You must edit the /etc/resolv.conf file and insert the IP addresses of your DNS servers. In the next screenshot, you can see the DNS configuration on the **node-1** cluster node:

```
[root@node-1 ~]# cat /etc/resolv.conf
nameserver 192.168.10.2
nameserver 192.168.10.3
```

You must also configure FQDN for the cluster nodes by editing the /etc/ sysconfig/network file and changing the HOSTNAME line to the FQDN of your cluster node. In the following screenshot, you can see the FQDN configuration of the **node-1** cluster node:

```
[root@node-1 ~]# cat /etc/sysconfig/network
NETWORKING=yes
HOSTNAME=node-1.geekpeek.net
```

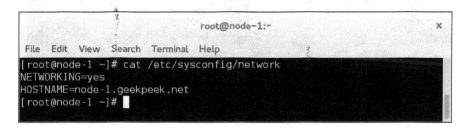

 Note that a cluster node reboot is required for hostname changes to take effect.

Edit the `/etc/hosts` file and add the IP address, followed by an FQDN and a short cluster node name, for every available cluster node network interface. In this screenshot, you can see the hosts file configuration for the **node-1** cluster node.

```
                              root@node-1:~                                   ×

 File  Edit  View  Search  Terminal  Help
[root@node-1 ~]# cat /etc/hosts
127.0.0.1     localhost localhost.localdomain localhost4 localhost4.localdomain4
::1           localhost localhost.localdomain localhost6 localhost6.localdomain6
192.168.88.10 node-1.geekpeek.net node-1
192.168.88.11 node-1.geekpeek.net node-1
192.168.88.20 node-2.geekpeek.net node-2
192.168.88.21 node-2.geekpeek.net node-2
192.168.88.30 node-3.geekpeek.net node-3
192.168.88.31 node-3.geekpeek.net node-3
[root@node-1 ~]#
```

You must configure DNS servers, and you must specify the fully qualified domain names in the `/etc/hosts` file on all cluster nodes. To complete this step, you must check and confirm connectivity among cluster nodes. You can simply do this by releasing a `ping` command to each cluster node. In the following screenshot, you can see the `ping` test performed from the **node-1** cluster node:

```
                              root@node-1:~                                   ×

 File  Edit  View  Search  Terminal  Help
[root@node-1 ~]# ping -c1 node-2
PING node-2.geekpeek.net (192.168.88.20) 56(84) bytes of data.
64 bytes from node-2.geekpeek.net (192.168.88.20): icmp_seq=1 ttl=64 time=0.747 ms

--- node-2.geekpeek.net ping statistics ---
1 packets transmitted, 1 received, 0% packet loss, time 0ms
rtt min/avg/max/mdev = 0.747/0.747/0.747/0.000 ms
[root@node-1 ~]# ping -c1 node-3
PING node-3.geekpeek.net (192.168.88.30) 56(84) bytes of data.
64 bytes from node-3.geekpeek.net (192.168.88.30): icmp_seq=1 ttl=64 time=0.034 ms

--- node-3.geekpeek.net ping statistics ---
1 packets transmitted, 1 received, 0% packet loss, time 0ms
rtt min/avg/max/mdev = 0.034/0.034/0.034/0.000 ms
[root@node-1 ~]#
```

You must check network connectivity among all cluster nodes and make sure that all **Internet Control Message Protocol (ICMP)** packets are transmitted and received and there is no packet loss.

Installing and configuring Corosync

Let's get down to business now. You must configure IPtables to allow cluster communication traffic among cluster nodes. You must add an `iptables` rule to allow UDP traffic on `5404` and `5405`, and another rule to allow multicast traffic communication. In this screenshot, you can see the commands to use for the `iptables` configuration:

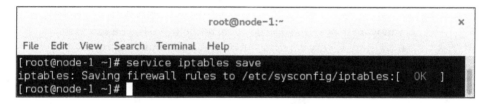

```
                              root@node-1:~                                    x

 File  Edit  View  Search  Terminal  Help
[root@node-1 ~]# iptables -I INPUT -m state --state NEW -p udp -m multiport --dports
5404,5405 -j ACCEPT
[root@node-1 ~]# iptables -I INPUT -m addrtype --dst-type MULTICAST -j ACCEPT
[root@node-1 ~]#
```

> The default Corosync cluster communication ports are `5404` and `5405`, and the UDP protocol is used. The ports are configured in the `/etc/corosync/corosync.conf` configuration file. If you want to change the default Corosync communication ports, make sure you change `iptables` accordingly.

Once you've run the commands, save the `iptables` configuration. In the following screenshot, you can see the command used to save the `iptables` configuration:

```
                              root@node-1:~                                    x

 File  Edit  View  Search  Terminal  Help
[root@node-1 ~]# service iptables save
iptables: Saving firewall rules to /etc/sysconfig/iptables:[  OK  ]
[root@node-1 ~]#
```

> You must add the IPTables rules and save the IPTables configuration on all cluster nodes. Then continue to install Corosync.

In this screenshot, you can see the command used to install Corosync:

```
                              root@node-1:~                                    x

 File  Edit  View  Search  Terminal  Help
[root@node-1 ~]# yum install corosync -y
```

You must install Corosync on all cluster nodes. You should generate the Corosync encryption keys with the `corosync-keygen` command to increase cluster security and encrypt cluster communication traffic. In the following screenshot, you can see the process of Corosync encryption key generation:

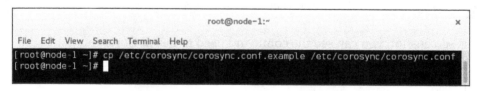

```
                              root@node-1:~                                  ×

 File   Edit   View   Search   Terminal   Help
[root@node-1 ~]# corosync-keygen
Corosync Cluster Engine Authentication key generator.
Gathering 1024 bits for key from /dev/random.
Press keys on your keyboard to generate entropy.
Press keys on your keyboard to generate entropy (bits = 152).
Press keys on your keyboard to generate entropy (bits = 216).
Press keys on your keyboard to generate entropy (bits = 280).
Press keys on your keyboard to generate entropy (bits = 344).
Press keys on your keyboard to generate entropy (bits = 408).
Press keys on your keyboard to generate entropy (bits = 472).
Press keys on your keyboard to generate entropy (bits = 536).
Press keys on your keyboard to generate entropy (bits = 600).
Press keys on your keyboard to generate entropy (bits = 664).
Press keys on your keyboard to generate entropy (bits = 728).
Press keys on your keyboard to generate entropy (bits = 792).
Press keys on your keyboard to generate entropy (bits = 856).
Press keys on your keyboard to generate entropy (bits = 920).
Press keys on your keyboard to generate entropy (bits = 984).
Writing corosync key to /etc/corosync/authkey.
[root@node-1 ~]#
```

 If you want to speed up the key generation process, you can use the `dd if=/dev/urandom of=file.txt` command, running in parallel with the `corosync-keygen` command. Stop the `dd` command when the key is generated, and delete the generated file.

Create a Corosync configuration file by copying it from sample configuration file. In this screenshot, you can see the use of the copy command:

```
                              root@node-1:~                                  ×

 File   Edit   View   Search   Terminal   Help
[root@node-1 ~]# cp /etc/corosync/corosync.conf.example /etc/corosync/corosync.conf
[root@node-1 ~]#
```

Edit the newly created Corosync configuration file and do the following:

1. Remove all commented-out lines — lines starting with # — and change the secauth parameter to on.

2. Change the `bindnetaddr` parameter to the current cluster node's IP address.

3. Change the to_syslog parameter to no. We will use a separate log file, so there's no need to duplicate the information in syslog.

Leave the rest of the parameters as they are. You can download the full Corosync configuration file from corosync-conf-1.txt.

The secauth parameter is used to encrypt cluster communication traffic, and it should be turned on. You must change the bindnetaddr parameter to the IP address of the cluster node you are currently on and the network interface you would like to use for cluster communication.

Change the to_syslog parameter to no if you want to avoid double logging. The default Corosync configuration logs /var/log/messages and /var/log/cluster/corosync.log log files.

Distribute the Corosync configuration file and the Corosync authkey file to other cluster nodes. In the following screenshot, you can see the files being distributed from the **node-1** cluster node using the scp command. For this command to be available on your system, the openssh-clients package must be installed first.

```
                              root@node-1:~                              ×

 File  Edit  View  Search  Terminal  Help
[root@node-1 ~]# scp /etc/corosync/corosync.conf node-2:/etc/corosync/
corosync.conf                          100%  421      0.4KB/s   00:00
[root@node-1 ~]# scp /etc/corosync/corosync.conf node-3:/etc/corosync/
corosync.conf                          100%  421      0.4KB/s   00:00
[root@node-1 ~]# scp /etc/corosync/authkey node-2:/etc/corosync/
authkey                                100%  128      0.1KB/s   00:00
[root@node-1 ~]# scp /etc/corosync/authkey node-3:/etc/corosync/
authkey                                100%  128      0.1KB/s   00:00
[root@node-1 ~]#
```

Once the Corosync configuration file has been transferred to other nodes, you must change the bindnetaddr parameter to the IP address of the cluster node you are editing the configuration file on.

Start the Corosync service. In this screenshot, you can see the command used to start the Corosync service on the **node-1** cluster node:

```
                              root@node-1:~                              ×

 File  Edit  View  Search  Terminal  Help
[root@node-1 ~]# service corosync start
Starting Corosync Cluster Engine (corosync):              [  OK  ]
[root@node-1 ~]#
```

You must start the Corosync service on all cluster nodes. You can check the Corosync membership status with the `corosync-objctl` command. In the following screenshot, you can see the command used to check the membership status:

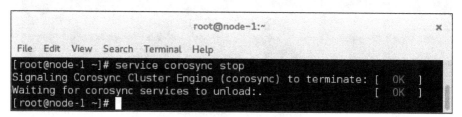

```
                              root@node-1:~                              x

  File  Edit  View  Search  Terminal  Help
[root@node-1 ~]# corosync-objctl |grep members
runtime.totem.pg.mrp.srp.members.173582528.ip=r(0) ip(192.168.88.10)
runtime.totem.pg.mrp.srp.members.173582528.join_count=1
runtime.totem.pg.mrp.srp.members.173582528.status=joined
runtime.totem.pg.mrp.srp.members.341354688.ip=r(0) ip(192.168.88.20)
runtime.totem.pg.mrp.srp.members.341354688.join_count=1
runtime.totem.pg.mrp.srp.members.341354688.status=joined
runtime.totem.pg.mrp.srp.members.509126848.ip=r(0) ip(192.168.88.30)
runtime.totem.pg.mrp.srp.members.509126848.join_count=1
runtime.totem.pg.mrp.srp.members.509126848.status=joined
[root@node-1 ~]#
```

 You can use the `grep` command to search for the `members` string in the `corosync-objctl` command output to get only the information you need.

As you can see, all three cluster node IP addresses should be listed. If they are, it means that all three cluster nodes have successfully joined the cluster. You can stop the Corosync service for now. In this screenshot, you can see the command used to stop the Corosync service:

```
                              root@node-1:~                              x

  File  Edit  View  Search  Terminal  Help
[root@node-1 ~]# service corosync stop
Signaling Corosync Cluster Engine (corosync) to terminate: [  OK  ]
Waiting for corosync services to unload:.                   [  OK  ]
[root@node-1 ~]#
```

 You must stop the Corosync service on all cluster nodes.

Installing and configuring CMAN

You're almost there! Continue by installing the CMAN software on your cluster nodes. In the following screenshot, you can see the command used to install the CMAN software on the **node-1** cluster node:

```
                              root@node-1:~                              ×
 File  Edit  View  Search  Terminal  Help
[root@node-1 ~]# yum install cman -y
```

You must install the CMAN software on all cluster nodes. Once you've installed CMAN, create a new file, /etc/cluster/cluster.conf, with your favorite text editor. In the next screenshot, you can see the lines you must insert into this file. You can also download the file from cman-conf-1.txt.

```
                              root@node-1:~                              ×
 File  Edit  View  Search  Terminal  Help
[root@node-1 ~]# cat /etc/cluster/cluster.conf
<?xml version="1.0"?>
<cluster config_version="1" name="hacluster">
  <logging debug="off"/>
  <clusternodes>
    <clusternode name="node-1" nodeid="1"/>
    <clusternode name="node-2" nodeid="2"/>
    <clusternode name="node-3" nodeid="3"/>
  </clusternodes>
</cluster>
[root@node-1 ~]#
```

The config_version parameter is the version of the CMAN configuration file, and the name parameter is your preferred cluster name.

The debug parameter is set to off and should be turned on for debugging purposes.

The clusternodes section is where the cluster nodes are configured. The clusternode parameter is defined by a name parameter, which is the FQDN or short node name, and the nodeid parameter, which is the ID of the cluster node.

Distribute the `/etc/cluster/cluster.conf` CMAN configuration file among all cluster nodes. The files are being distributed from the **node-1** cluster node using the `scp` command. For this command to be available on your system, the `openssh-clients` package must be installed first. Take a look at the following screenshot:

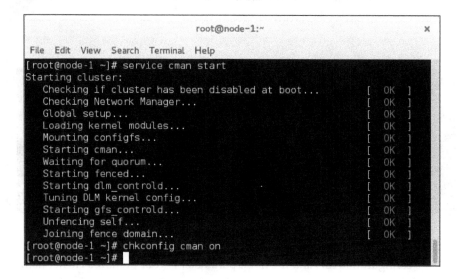

Start the CMAN service, and make it start at boot. In this screenshot, you can see the command used to start the CMAN service and the service start process, and the command to make CMAN start at boot:

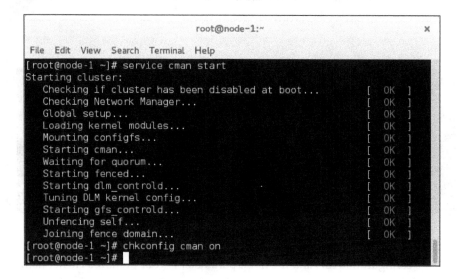

 You must start the CMAN service and make it start at boot on all cluster nodes.

Once the CMAN service has been successfully started on all cluster nodes, check the CMAN node status using the `cman_tool nodes` command. All three cluster nodes should be listed with status as **M**. In the following screenshot, you can see the output of the `cman_tool nodes` command issued on the **node-1** cluster node:

```
                          root@node-1:~                         ×
 File  Edit  View  Search  Terminal  Help
[root@node-1 ~]# cman_tool nodes
Node  Sts   Inc   Joined                    Name
   1   M    860   2015-03-01 22:00:47       node-1
   2   M    864   2015-03-01 22:00:47       node-2
   3   M    864   2015-03-01 22:00:47       node-3
[root@node-1 ~]#
```

Let's take a look at each column in more detail:

- **Node**: This column shows the node ID number.

- **Sts**: This column shows the cluster node status, with **M** indicating that the node is a joined cluster member and **X** indicating that the node is dead.

- **Inc**: This column is for debugging purposes only. It is the incarnation number.

- **Joined**: This column shows the time the cluster member joined the cluster.

- **Name**: This column shows the cluster node name as defined in the cluster. conf file.

You should also check the Quorum status with the cman_tool status command. In the following screenshot, you can see the output of the cman_tool status command issued on the **node-1** cluster node:

```
                          root@node-1:~                         ×
 File  Edit  View  Search  Terminal  Help
[root@node-1 ~]# cman_tool status
Version: 6.2.0
Config Version: 32
Cluster Name: hacluster
Cluster Id: 10117
Cluster Member: Yes
Cluster Generation: 864
Membership state: Cluster-Member
Nodes: 3
Expected votes: 3
Total votes: 3
Node votes: 1
Quorum: 2
Active subsystems: 7
Flags:
Ports Bound: 0
Node name: node-1
Node ID: 1
Multicast addresses: 239.192.39.172
Node addresses: 192.168.88.10
[root@node-1 ~]#
```

- **Nodes**: This line is where the number of your cluster nodes should be listed
- **Expected votes**: This line shows the number of expected votes in the currently active configuration
- **Total votes**: This line shows the number of total votes provided by the CMAN configuration file
- **Node votes**: This line shows the number of votes the current node has
- **Quorum**: This line shows the number of votes required to reach Quorum

The finishing touch for the CMAN installation and configuration process is the start of a service called `ricci`. The `ricci` service provides on-the-fly CMAN configuration file distribution. In the following screenshot, you can see the command used to start the `ricci` service and also the command used to make it start at boot:

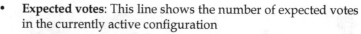

```
root@node-1:~                                           ×
File  Edit  View  Search  Terminal  Help
[root@node-1 ~]# service ricci start
Starting ricci:                                      [  OK  ]
[root@node-1 ~]# chkconfig ricci on
[root@node-1 ~]#
```

Installing and configuring RGManager

Now for the finishing touch; first, add the `iptables` rule to allow RGManager, DLM, and Ricci traffic. In this screenshot, you can see the command used to allow RGManager and DLM traffic issued on the **node-1** cluster node:

```
root@node-1:~                                           ×
File  Edit  View  Search  Terminal  Help
[root@node-1 ~]# iptables -I INPUT -m state --state NEW -p tcp -m multiport
 --dports 11111,21064,41966,41967,41968,41969 -j ACCEPT
[root@node-1 ~]#
```

You must save the `iptables` configuration. In the following screenshot, you can see the command used to save the `iptables` configuration:

```
                          root@node-1:~                              ×

 File   Edit   View   Search   Terminal   Help
[root@node-1 ~]# service iptables save
iptables: Saving firewall rules to /etc/sysconfig/iptables:[  OK  ]
[root@node-1 ~]#
```

Continue by installing RGManager, starting the RGManager service, and making it start at boot. In this screenshot, you can see the command used to install the RGManager service on the **node-1** cluster node:

```
                          root@node-1:~                              ×

 File   Edit   View   Search   Terminal   Help
[root@node-1 ~]# yum install rgmanager -y
```

In the following screenshot, you can see the commands used to start the RGManager service and make RGManager start at boot on the **node-1** cluster node:

```
                          root@node-1:~                              ×

 File   Edit   View   Search   Terminal   Help
[root@node-1 ~]# service rgmanager start
Starting Cluster Service Manager:                        [  OK  ]
[root@node-1 ~]# chkconfig rgmanager on
[root@node-1 ~]#
```

You must add an iptables rule, save the iptables configuration, and install and start the RGManager service on all cluster nodes. Do not forget to make RGManager start at boot. You can now check the cluster status using the clustat command. In this screenshot, you can see the clustat command issued on the **node-1** cluster node and the output it gives:

```
                          root@node-1:~                              ×

 File   Edit   View   Search   Terminal   Help
[root@node-1 ~]# clustat
Cluster Status for hacluster @ Sun Mar  1 22:18:02 2015
Member Status: Quorate

 Member Name                         ID   Status
 ------ ----                         ---- ------
 node-1                              1 Online, Local, rgmanager
 node-2                              2 Online, rgmanager
 node-3                              3 Online, rgmanager
```

- **Member status**: This line provides information about the Quorum status.
- **Member Name**: This column shows the cluster node name as defined in the `cluster.conf` configuration file.
- **ID**: This column shows the node ID number.
- **Status**: This column provides information about the node's status. The output of the `clustat` command must list all the cluster nodes as online, confirming that installation and configuration of the cluster stack software on CentOS 6 were successful and that you did a great job at it.

Downloading the example code

You can download the example code files for all Packt books you have purchased from your account at http://www.packtpub.com. If you purchased this book elsewhere, you can visit http://www.packtpub.com/support and register to have the files e-mailed directly to you.

Summary

This chapter provided information on how to prepare the operating system for the installation of cluster stack software and also the steps required for this installation. It guided you through the process of installing and configuring Corosync and the CMAN cluster messaging layer software, and ended with the steps for installing and configuring RGManager cluster resource management. The next chapter will explore in greater depth using RGManager to configure and manage different sorts of cluster resources and services.

4

Resource Manager on CentOS 6

This chapter will cover cluster resource management on CentOS 6 with the RGManager cluster resource manager. You will learn how and where to find the information you require about the cluster resources that are supported by RGManager, and all the details about cluster resource configuration. You will also learn how to add, delete, and reconfigure resources and services in your cluster. Then you will learn how to start, stop, and migrate resources from one cluster node to another. When you are done with this chapter, your cluster will be configured to run and provide end users with a service.

Working with RGManager

When we work with RGManager, the cluster resources are configured within the `/etc/cluster/cluster.conf` CMAN configuration file. RGManager has a dedicated section in the CMAN configuration file defined by the `<rm>` tag. Part of configuration within the `<rm>` tag belongs to RGManager. The RGManager section begins with the `<rm>` tag and ends with the `</rm>` tag. This syntax is common for XML files.

The RGManager section must be defined within the `<cluster>` section of the CMAN configuration file but not within the `<clusternodes>` or `<fencedevices>` sections. We will be able to review the exact configuration syntax from the example configuration file provided in the next paragraphs.

The following elements can be used within the `<rm>` RGManager tag:

- **Failover Domain: (tag: <failoverdomains></failoverdomains>)**: A failover domain is a set of cluster nodes that are eligible to run a specific cluster service in the event of a cluster node failure. More than one failure domain can be configured with different rules applied for different cluster services.

- **Global Resources: (tag: <resources></resources>)**: Global cluster resources are globally configured resources that can be related when configuring cluster services. Global cluster resources simplify the process of cluster service configuration by global resource name reference.

- **Cluster Service: (tag: <service></service>)**: A cluster service usually defines more than one resource combined to provide a cluster service. The order of resources provided within a cluster service is important because it defines the resource start and stop order.

The most used and important RGManager command-line expressions are as follows:

- `clustat`: The `clustat` command provides cluster status information. It also provides information about the cluster, cluster nodes, and cluster services.

- `clusvcadm`: The `clusvcadm` command provides cluster service management commands such as start, stop, disable, enable, relocate, and others.

By default, RGManager logging is configured to log information related to RGManager to the syslog `/var/log/messages` file. If the `logfile` parameter in the Corosync configuration file's logging section is configured, information related to RGManager will be logged in the location specified by the `logfile` parameter. The default RGManager log file is named `rgmanager.log`.

Let's start with the details of RGManager configuration.

Configuring failover domains

The `<rm>` tag in the CMAN configuration file usually begins with the definition of a failover domain, but configuring a failover domain is not required for normal operation of the cluster.

A failover domain is a set of cluster nodes with configured failover rules. The failover domain is attached to the cluster service configuration; in the event of a cluster node failure, the configured cluster service's failover domain rules are applied.

Failover domains are configured within the `<rm>` RGManager tag. The failover domain configuration begins with the `<failoverdomains>` tag and ends with the `</failoverdomains>` tag. Within the `<failoverdomains>` tag, you can specify one or more failover domains in the following form:

```
<failoverdomain failoverdomainname failoverdomain_options>
</failoverdomain>
```

The `failoverdomainname` parameter is a unique name provided for the failover domain in the form of `name="desired_name"`.

The `failoverdomain_options` options are the rules that we apply to the failover domain.

The following rules can be configured for a failover domain:

- **Unrestricted: (parameter: restricted="0")**: This failover domain configuration allows you to run a cluster service on any of the configured cluster nodes.

- **Restricted: (parameter: restricted="1")**: This failover domain configuration allows you to restrict a cluster service to run on the members you configure.

- **Ordered: (parameter: ordered="1")**: This failover domain configuration allows you to configure a preference order for cluster nodes. In the event of cluster node failure, the preference order is taken into account. The order of the listed cluster nodes is important because it is also the priority order.

- **Unordered: (parameter: ordered="0")**: This failover domain configuration allows any of the configured cluster nodes to run a specific cluster service.

- **Failback: (parameter: nofailback="0")**: This failover domain configuration allows you to configure failback for the cluster service. This means the cluster service will fail back to the originating cluster node once the cluster node is operational.

- **Nofailback: (parameter: nofailback="1")**: This failover domain configuration allows you to disable the failback of the cluster service back to the originating cluster node once it is operational.

Within the `<failoverdomain>` tag, the desired cluster nodes are configured with a `<failoverdomainnode>` tag in the following form:

```
<failoverdomainnode nodename/>
```

 The nodename parameter is the cluster node name as provided in the `<clusternode>` tag of the CMAN configuration file.

Continuing with the configuration example from the previous chapter, you can add the following simple failover domain configuration to your existing CMAN configuration file. In the following screenshot, you can see the CMAN configuration file with a simple failover domain configuration. You can download the CMAN configuration file from the `cman-conf-1.txt` file in the code bundle.

```
root@node-1:~                                    x
File  Edit  View  Search  Terminal  Help
[root@node-1 ~]# cat /etc/cluster/cluster.conf
<?xml version="1.0"?>
<cluster config_version="2" name="hacluster">
  <logging debug="off"/>
  <clusternodes>
    <clusternode name="node-1" nodeid="1"/>
    <clusternode name="node-2" nodeid="2"/>
    <clusternode name="node-3" nodeid="3"/>
  </clusternodes>
  <rm>
    <failoverdomains>
      <failoverdomain name="simple" nofailback="1" ordered="0" restricted="0">
        <failoverdomainnode name="node-1"/>
        <failoverdomainnode name="node-2"/>
        <failoverdomainnode name="node-3"/>
      </failoverdomain>
    </failoverdomains>
  </rm>
</cluster>
[root@node-1 ~]# 
```

The previous example shows a failover domain named `simple` with no failback, no ordering, and no restrictions configured. All three cluster nodes are listed as failover domain nodes.

Note that it is important to change the `config_version` parameter in the second line on every CMAN cluster configuration file.

Once you have configured the failover domain, you need to validate the cluster configuration file. A valid CMAN configuration is required for normal operation of the cluster. If the validation of the cluster configuration file fails, recheck the configuration file for common typo errors. In the following screenshot, you can see the command used to check the CMAN configuration file for errors:

```
root@node-1:~                                    x
File  Edit  View  Search  Terminal  Help
[root@node-1 ~]# ccs_config_validate
Configuration validates
[root@node-1 ~]# 
```

Note that, if a specific cluster node is not online, the configuration file will have to be transferred manually and the cluster stack software will have to be restarted to catch up once it comes back online.

Once your configuration is validated, you can propagate it to other cluster nodes. In this screenshot, you can see the CMAN configuration file propagation command used on the **node-1** cluster node:

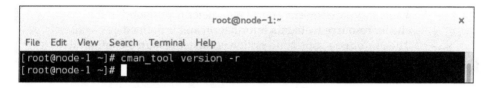

 For successful CMAN configuration file distribution to the other cluster nodes, the CMAN configuration file's `config_version` parameter number must be increased.

You can confirm that the configuration file was successfully distributed by issuing the `ccs_config_dump` command on any of the other cluster nodes and comparing the XML output.

Adding cluster resources and services

The difference between cluster resources and cluster services is that a cluster service is a service built from one or more cluster resources. A configured cluster resource is prepared to be used within a cluster service. When you are configuring a cluster service, you reference a configured cluster resource by its unique name.

Resources

Cluster resources are defined within the `<rm>` RGManager tag of the CMAN configuration file. They begin with the `<resources>` tag and end with the `</resources>` tag. Within the `<resources>` tag, all cluster resources supported by RGManager can be configured.

Cluster resources are configured with resource scripts, and all RGManager-supported resource scripts are located in the `/usr/share/cluster` directory along with the cluster resource metadata information required to configure a cluster resource. For some cluster resources, the metadata information is listed within the cluster resource scripts, while others have separate cluster resource metadata files.

RGManager reads metadata from the scripts while validating the CMAN configuration file. Therefore, knowing the metadata information is the best way to correctly define and configure a cluster resource.

The basic syntax used to configure a cluster resource is as follows:

```
<resource_agent_name resource_options"/>
```

 The `resource_agent_name` parameter is provided in the cluster resource metadata information and is defined as name. The `resource_options` option is cluster resource-configurable options as provided in the cluster resource metadata information.

If you want to configure an IP address cluster resource, you should first review the IP address of the cluster resource metadata information, which is available in the `/usr/share/cluster/ip.sh` script file.

The syntax used to define an IP address cluster resource is as follows:

```
<ip ip_address_options/>
```

We can configure a simple `IPv4` IP address, such as `192.168.88.50`, and bind it to the `eth1` network interface by adding the following line to the CMAN configuration:

```
<ip address="192.168.88.50" family="IPv4" prefer_interface="eth1"/>
```

 The `address` option is the IP address you want to configure. The `family` option is the address protocol family. The `prefer_interface` option binds the IP address to the specific network interface.

By reviewing the IP address of resource metadata information we can see that a few additional options are configurable and well explained:

- monitor_link
- nfslock
- sleeptime
- disable_rdisc

If you want to configure an Apache web server cluster resource, you should first review the Apache web server resource's metadata information in the `/usr/share/cluster/apache.metadata` metadata file.

The syntax used to define an Apache web server cluster resource is as follows:

```
<apache apache_web_server_options/>
```

We can configure a simple Apache web server cluster resource by adding the following line to the CMAN configuration file:

```
<apache name="apache" server_root="/etc/httpd" config_file="conf/httpd.
conf" shutdown_wait="60"/>
```

> The name parameter is the unique name provided for the apache cluster resource.
>
> The server_root option provides the Apache installation location. If no server_root option is provided, the default value is /etc/httpd.
>
> The config_file option is the path to the main Apache web server configuration file from the server_root file. If no config_file option is provided, the default value is conf/httpd.conf.
>
> The shutdown_wait option is the number of seconds to wait before the correct end-of-service shutdown.

By reviewing the Apache web server resource metadata, you can see that a few additional options are configurable and well explained:

- httpd
- httpd_options
- service_name

We can add the IP address and Apache web server cluster resources to the example configuration we are building, as follows. The full CMAN configuration file is available for download from the following cman-conf-2.txt file in the code bundle:

```
<resources>
  <ip address="192.168.10.50" family="IPv4"
  prefer_interface="eth1"/>
  <apache name="apache" server_root="/etc/httpd"
  config_file="conf/httpd.conf" shutdown_wait="60"/>
</resources>
```

> Do not forget to increase the config_version parameter number.

Make sure that you the validate cluster configuration file with every change. In the following screenshot, you can see the command used to validate the CMAN configuration:

```
root@node-1:~                                    ×
 File  Edit  View  Search  Terminal  Help
[root@node-1 ~]# ccs_config_validate
Configuration validates
[root@node-1 ~]#
```

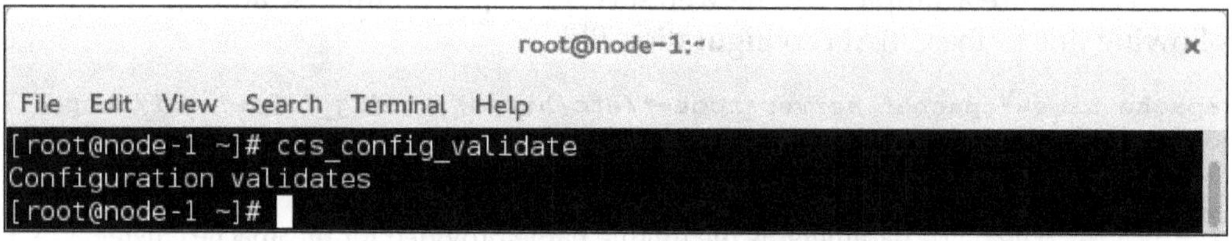

After we've validated our configuration, we can distribute the cluster configuration file to other nodes. In this screenshot, you can see the command used to distribute the CMAN configuration file from the **node-1** cluster node to other cluster nodes:

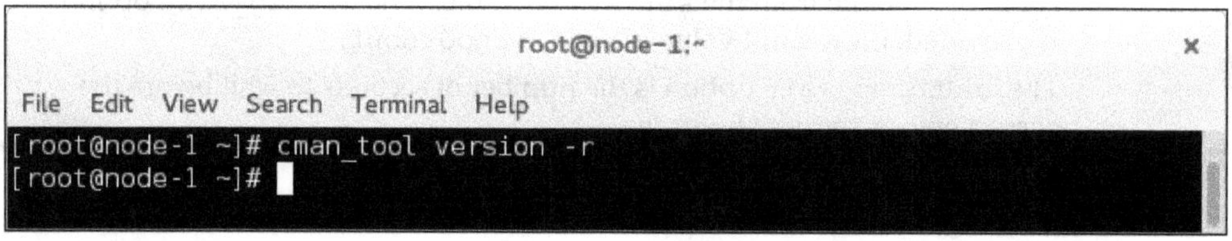

```
root@node-1:~                                    ×
 File  Edit  View  Search  Terminal  Help
[root@node-1 ~]# cman_tool version -r
[root@node-1 ~]#
```

Services

The cluster services are defined within the `<rm>` RGManager tag of the CMAN configuration file after the cluster resources tag. They begin with the `<service>` tag and end with the `</service>` tag.

The syntax used to define a service is as follows:

```
<service service_options>
</service>
```

The resources within the cluster services are referenced to the globally configured cluster resources. The order of the cluster resources configured within the cluster service is important. This is because it is also a resource start order. The syntax for cluster resource configuration within the cluster service is as follows:

```
<service service_options>
  <resource_agent_name ref="referenced_cluster_resource_name"/>
</service>
```

The service options can be the following:

- **Autostart: (parameter: autostart="1")**: This parameter starts services when RGManager starts. By default, RGManager starts all services when it is started and Quorum is present.

- **Noautostart (parameter: autostart="0")**: This parameter disables the start of all services when RGManager starts.

- **Restart recovery (parameter: recovery="restart")**: This is RGManager's default recovery policy. On failure, RGManager will restart the service on the same cluster node. If the service restart fails, RGManager will relocate the service to another operational cluster node.

- **Relocate recovery (parameter: recovery="relocate")**: On failure, RGManager will try to start the service on other operational cluster nodes.

- **Disable recovery (parameter: recovery="disable")**: On failure RGManager, will place the service in the disabled state.

- **Restart disable recovery (parameter: recovery="restart-disable")**: On failure, RGManager will try to restart the service on the same cluster node. If the restart fails, it will place the service in the disabled state.

Additional restart policy extensions are available, as follows:

- **Maximum restarts (parameter: max_restarts="N"; where N is the desired integer value)**: the maximum restarts parameter is defined by an integer that specifies the maximum number of service restarts before taking additional recovery policy actions

- **Restart expire time (parameter: restart_expire_time="N"; where N is the desired integer value in seconds)**: The restart expire time parameter is defined by an integer value in seconds, and configures the time to remember a restart event

We can configure a web server cluster service with respect to the configured IP address and Apache web server resources with the following CMAN configuration file syntax:

```
<service name="webserver" autostart="1" recovery="relocate">
  <ip ref="192.168.88.50"/>
  <apache ref="apache"/>
</service>
```

A minimal configuration of a web server cluster service requires a cluster IP address and an Apache web server resource.

- The `name` parameter defines a unique name for the web server cluster service.
- The `autostart` parameter defines an automatic start of the webserver cluster service on RGManager startup.
- The `recovery` parameter configures the restart of the web server cluster service on other cluster nodes in the event of failure.

We can add the web server cluster service to the example CMAN configuration file we are building, as follows. The full CMAN configuration file is available for download from `cman-conf-3.txt`:

```
<resources>

  <ip address="192.168.10.50" family="IPv4"
  prefer_interface="eth1"/>

  <apache name="apache" server_root="/etc/httpd"
  config_file="conf/httpd.conf" shutdown_wait="60"/>

</resources>

<service name="webserver" autostart="1" recovery="relocate">

  <ip ref="192.168.10.50"/>

  <apache ref="apache"/>

</service>
```

Do not forget to increase the `config_version` parameter.

Make sure you validate the cluster configuration file with every change. In the following screenshot, we can see the command used to validate the CMAN configuration:

```
root@node-1:~                                          ×

File  Edit  View  Search  Terminal  Help
[root@node-1 ~]# ccs_config_validate
Configuration validates
[root@node-1 ~]#
```

After you've validated your configuration, you can distribute the cluster configuration file to other nodes. In this screenshot, we can see the command used to distribute the CMAN configuration file from the **node-1** cluster node to other cluster nodes:

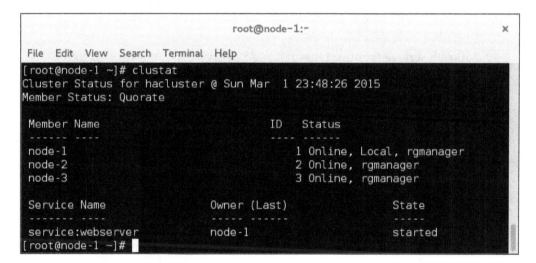

```
root@node-1:~                                        ×

File   Edit   View   Search   Terminal   Help
[root@node-1 ~]# cman_tool version -r
[root@node-1 ~]#
```

With the final distribution of the cluster configuration, a cluster service is configured and RGManager starts the cluster service called `webserver`. You can use the `clustat` command to check whether the web server cluster service was successfully started and also which cluster node it is running on. In the following screenshot, you can see the `clustat` command issued on the **node-1** cluster node:

```
root@node-1:~                                        ×

File   Edit   View   Search   Terminal   Help
[root@node-1 ~]# clustat
Cluster Status for hacluster @ Sun Mar  1 23:48:26 2015
Member Status: Quorate

 Member Name                        ID   Status
 ------ ----                        ---- ------
 node-1                              1 Online, Local, rgmanager
 node-2                              2 Online, rgmanager
 node-3                              3 Online, rgmanager

 Service Name               Owner (Last)               State
 ------- ----               ----- ------               -----
 service:webserver          node-1                     started
[root@node-1 ~]#
```

Let's take a look at the following terms:

- **Service Name**: This column defines the name of the service as configured in the CMAN configuration file.
- **Owner**: This column lists the node the service is running on or was last running on.
- **State**: This column provides information about the status of the service.

Managing cluster services

Once you have configured the cluster services as you like, you must learn how to manage them. We can manage cluster services with the `clusvcadm` command and additional parameters. The syntax of the `clusvcadm` command is as follows:

```
clusvcadm [parameter]
```

With the `clusvcadm` command, you can perform the following actions:

- **Disable service (syntax: clusvcadm -d <service_name>)**: This stops the cluster service and puts it into the disabled state. This is the only permitted operation if the service in question is in the failed state.

- **Start service (syntax: clusvcadm -e <service_name> -m <cluster_node>)**: This starts a non-running cluster service. It optionally provides the cluster node name you would like to start the service on.

- **Relocate service (syntax: clusvcadm -r <service_name> -m <cluster_node>)**: This stops the cluster service and starts it on a different cluster node as provided with the -m parameter.

- **Migrate service (syntax: clusvcadm -M <service_name> -m <cluster_node>)**: Note that this applies only to virtual machine live migrations.

- **Restart service (syntax: clusvcadm -R <service_name>)**: This stops and starts a cluster service on the same cluster node.

- **Stop service (syntax: clusvcadm -s <service_name>)**: This stops the cluster service and keeps it on the current cluster node in the stopped state.

- **Freeze service (syntax: clusvcadm -Z <service_name>)**: This keeps the cluster service running on the current cluster node but disables service status checks and service failover in the event of a cluster node failure.

- **Unfreeze service (syntax: clusvcadm -U <service_name>)**: This takes the cluster service out of the frozen state and enables service status checks and failover.

We can continue with the previous example and migrate the `webserver` cluster service from the currently running **node-1** cluster node to the `node-3` cluster node. To achieve cluster service relocation, the `clusvcadm` command with the relocate service parameter must be used, as follows. In the following screenshot, we can see the command issued to migrate the `webserver` cluster service to the `node-3` cluster node:

```
                              root@node-1:~                              ×

File  Edit  View  Search  Terminal  Help
[root@node-1 ~]# clusvcadm -r webserver -m node-3
Trying to relocate service:webserver to node-3...Success
service:webserver is now running on node-3
[root@node-1 ~]# █
```

The clusvcadm command is the cluster service command used to administer and manage cluster services.

The -r webserver parameter provides information that we need to relocate a cluster service named webserver.

The -m node-3 command provides information on where we want to relocate the cluster service.

Once the cluster service migration command completes, the webserver cluster service will be relocated to the node-3 cluster node. The clustat command shows that the webserver service is now running on the node-3 cluster node. In this screenshot, we can see that the webserver cluster service was successfully relocated to the node-3 cluster node:

```
                              root@node-1:~                              ×

File  Edit  View  Search  Terminal  Help
[root@node-1 ~]# clustat
Cluster Status for hacluster @ Sun Mar  1 23:56:03 2015
Member Status: Quorate

Member Name                        ID    Status
------ ----                        ----  ------
node-1                             1 Online, Local, rgmanager
node-2                             2 Online, rgmanager
node-3                             3 Online, rgmanager

Service Name              Owner (Last)                   State
------- ----              ----- ------                   -----
service:webserver         node-3                         started
[root@node-1 ~]# █
```

We can easily stop the `webserver` cluster service by issuing the appropriate command. In the following screenshot, we can see the command used to stop the `webserver` cluster service:

```
                              root@node-1:~                              ×

 File  Edit  View  Search  Terminal  Help
[root@node-1 ~]# clusvcadm -s webserver
Local machine stopping service:webserver...Success
[root@node-1 ~]# 
```

The `clusvcadm` command is the cluster service command used to administer and manage cluster services.

The `-s webserver` parameter provides the information that you require to stop a cluster service named `webserver`. Another take at the `clustat` command should show that the `webserver` cluster service has stopped; it also provides the information that the last owner of the running `webserver` cluster service is the `node-3` cluster node.

In this screenshot, we can see the output of the `clustat` command, showing that the `webserver` cluster service is running on the **node-3** cluster node:

```
                              root@node-1:~                              ×

 File  Edit  View  Search  Terminal  Help
[root@node-1 ~]# clustat
Cluster Status for hacluster @ Mon Mar  2 00:02:03 2015
Member Status: Quorate

 Member Name                         ID   Status
 ------ ----                         ---- ------
 node-1                                 1 Online, Local, rgmanager
 node-2                                 2 Online, rgmanager
 node-3                                 3 Online, rgmanager

 Service Name              Owner (Last)                     State
 ------- ----              ----- ------                     -----
 service:webserver         (node-3)                         stopped
[root@node-1 ~]# 
```

If we want to start the webserver cluster service on the **node-1** cluster node, we can do this by issuing the appropriate command. In the following screenshot, we can see the command used to start the webserver cluster service on the **node-1** cluster node:

```
                              root@node-1:~                              ×
 File  Edit  View  Search  Terminal  Help
[root@node-1 ~]# clusvcadm -e webserver -m node-1
Member node-1 trying to enable service:webserver...Success
service:webserver is now running on node-1
[root@node-1 ~]#
```

clusvcadm is the cluster service command used to administer and manage cluster services.

The -e webserver parameter provides the information that you need to start a webserver cluster service.

The -m node-1 parameter provides the information that you need to start the webserver cluster service on the **node-1** cluster node. As expected, another look at the clustat command should make it clear that the webserver cluster service has started on the **node-1** cluster node, as follows.

In this screenshot, you can see the output of the clustat command, showing that the webserver cluster service is running on the **node -1** cluster node:

```
                              root@node-1:~                              ×
 File  Edit  View  Search  Terminal  Help
[root@node-1 ~]# clustat
Cluster Status for hacluster @ Mon Mar  2 00:06:40 2015
Member Status: Quorate

 Member Name                        ID    Status
 ------ ----                        ----  ------
 node-1                             1 Online, Local, rgmanager
 node-2                             2 Online, rgmanager
 node-3                             3 Online, rgmanager

 Service Name           Owner (Last)                  State
 -------- ----          ----- ------                  -----
 service:webserver      node-1                        started
[root@node-1 ~]#
```

Removing cluster resources and services

Removing cluster resources and services is the reverse of adding them. Resources and services are removed by editing the CMAN configuration file and removing the lines that define the resources or services you would like to remove. When removing cluster resources, it is important to verify that the resources are not being used within any of the configured or running cluster services. As always, when editing the CMAN configuration file, the config_version parameter must be increased. Once the CMAN configuration file is edited, you must run the CMAN configuration validation check for errors. When the CMAN configuration file validation succeeds, you can distribute it to all other cluster nodes.

The procedure for removing cluster resources and services is as follows:

1. Remove the desired cluster resources and services and increase the config_version number.
2. Validate the CMAN configuration file.
3. Distribute the CMAN configuration file to all other nodes.

We can proceed to remove the webserver cluster service from our example cluster configuration. Edit the CMAN configuration file and remove the webserver cluster service definition. We can download the full CMAN configuration file, with the webserver cluster service removed, from cman-conf-4.txt.

 Remember to increase the config_version number. Validate your cluster configuration with every CMAN configuration file change.

In this screenshot, we can see the command used to validate the CMAN configuration:

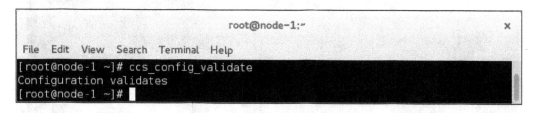

When your cluster configuration is valid, you can distribute the CMAN configuration file to all other cluster nodes. In the following screenshot, we can see the command used to distribute the CMAN configuration file from the **node-1** cluster node to other cluster nodes:

```
root@node-1:~                                          ×
File   Edit   View   Search   Terminal   Help
[root@node-1 ~]# cman_tool version -r
[root@node-1 ~]#
```

Once the cluster configuration is distributed to all cluster nodes, the webserver cluster service will be stopped and removed. The clustat command shows no service configured and running. In the following screenshot, we can see that the output of the clustat command shows no cluster service called webserver existing in the cluster:

```
root@node-1:~                                          ×
File   Edit   View   Search   Terminal   Help
[root@node-1 ~]# clustat
Cluster Status for hacluster @ Mon Mar  2 00:28:45 2015
Member Status: Quorate

 Member Name                          ID   Status
 ------ ----                          ---- ------
 node-1                               1 Online, Local
 node-2                               2 Online
 node-3                               3 Online

[root@node-1 ~]#
```

Summary

In this chapter, you learned how to add and remove cluster failover domains, cluster resources, and cluster services. You also learned how to start, stop, and migrate cluster services from one cluster node to another, and how to remove cluster resources and services from a running cluster configuration. In the next chapter, we will start playing with cluster nodes. You will learn how to add and remove cluster nodes from your cluster configuration.

5
Playing with Cluster Nodes on CentOS 6

In the previous chapter, you learned how to add, manage, and remove failover domains, cluster resources, and cluster services with RGManager on CentOS 6. Since a computer cluster is a live system and is constantly developing and growing with additional resources and services, it is also very important for you, as a cluster administrator, to know how to add or remove a cluster node from the cluster if the situation requires you to.

This chapter focuses on familiarizing you with cluster node management on CentOS 6. You will learn how to add and remove cluster nodes from an existing and running computer cluster.

Adding a new cluster node

Adding a new cluster node to an existing cluster configuration does not require any cluster service downtime. By this point, you should be familiar with the process of installing and configuring cluster stack software on a new CentOS 6 cluster node, so the steps for adding a new cluster node are not covered in detail.

To add a new cluster node to the existing cluster configuration, follow these steps:

1. Operating system preparation:

    ° Configure network interfaces and networking
    ° Configure NTP time synchronization
    ° Configure DNS resolving
    ° Check the network connectivity between the cluster nodes

For a detailed procedure on operating system preparation on CentOS 6, refer to *Chapter 3, Cluster Stack Software on CentOS 6*.

2. Install and configure Corosync:

   ○ Install Corosync on the new cluster node and configure `iptables` rules to allow Corosync cluster communication.

   ○ Transfer the `corosync.conf` configuration file and the `authkey` authentication key from one of the preexisting cluster nodes to the new cluster node. In the following screenshot, you can see the `scp` command used to transfer the `corosync.conf` configuration file and the `authkey` authentication key to the `node-4.geekpeek.net` cluster node:

```
                              root@node-1:~                                    ✕

 File   Edit   View   Search   Terminal   Help
[root@node-1 ~]# scp /etc/corosync/corosync.conf node-4:/etc/corosync/
corosync.conf                            100%   421      0.4KB/s   00:00
[root@node-1 ~]# scp /etc/corosync/authkey node-4:/etc/corosync/
authkey                                  100%   128      0.1KB/s   00:00
[root@node-1 ~]#
```

   ○ Edit the Corosync configuration file on the new cluster node and change the `bindnetaddr` parameter accordingly. You can download an example `corosync.conf` configuration file from the `corosync-conf-1.txt` file in the code bundle.

   ○ The `bindnetaddr` parameter must be changed to the `node-4.geekpeek.net` cluster node's IP address.

 For a detailed discussion of Corosync installation and configuration on CentOS 6, refer to *Chapter 3, Cluster Stack Software on CentOS 6*.

3. Install and configure CMAN and Ricci:

   ○ Install CMAN and Ricci and configure the `iptables` rules to allow Ricci cluster communication.

   ○ Start Ricci on the new cluster node. In the following screenshot, you can see the command used to start Ricci on the **node-4** cluster node:

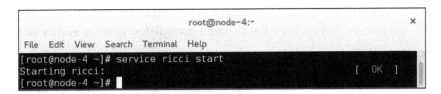

- ○ Edit the CMAN configuration file on one of the pre-existing cluster nodes, and add a new cluster node to the `<clusternodes>` section and the `<failoverdomains>` section, if required. Do not forget to increase the `config_version` parameter number. You can download an example CMAN `cluster.conf` configuration file from the `cman-conf-2.txt` file in the code bundle.

- ○ A new cluster node called `node-4` is now added to the cluster configuration within the `<clusternodes>` and `<failoverdomains>` sections.

- ○ Verify the cluster configuration and distribute the new cluster configuration to all other cluster nodes as follows. In the following screenshot, you can see the command used to verify the cluster configuration and propagate it to other cluster nodes:

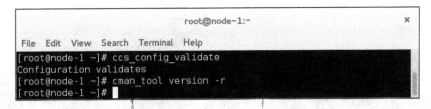

- ○ The CMAN `cluster.conf` configuration file is now successfully distributed at the new **node-4** cluster node due to the running Ricci service.

- ○ Start the CMAN service on the new cluster node and check the cluster node's status with the `cman_tool nodes` command. In the following screenshot, you can see the output of the `cman_tool nodes` command:

```
root@node-4:~                                          ×

File  Edit  View  Search  Terminal  Help
[root@node-4 ~]# cman_tool nodes
Node  Sts   Inc   Joined               Name
   1   M    920   2015-03-06 20:49:27  node-1
   2   M    920   2015-03-06 20:49:27  node-2
   3   M    920   2015-03-06 20:49:27  node-3
   4   M    580   2015-03-06 20:49:27  node-4
[root@node-4 ~]#
```

Here, you can also see that the new **node-4** cluster node has successfully joined the cluster and is listed with its status as **M**.

4. Install and configure RGManager:

   ○ Install RGManager and configure the `iptables` rules to allow RGManager traffic.

   ○ Start RGmanager on the new cluster node, as shown in the following screenshot:

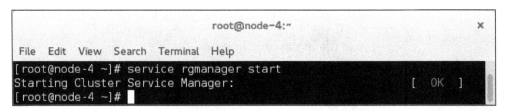

   ○ Check the cluster status and confirm that all cluster nodes are listed as expected. In the following screenshot, you can see the output of the `clustat` command, confirming that the **node-4** cluster node has successfully joined the cluster:

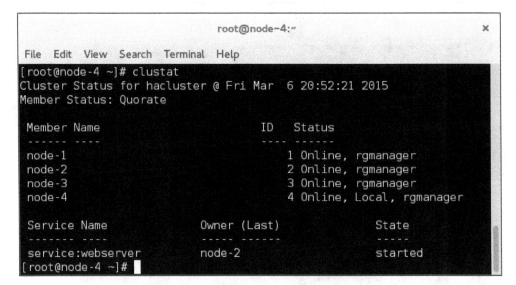

Removing a cluster node

Removing a cluster node from an existing cluster configuration is easy, and is done by turning it off and editing the CMAN configuration file on existing cluster nodes. You can also just stop the cluster stack software services on the node you want to remove from a cluster. Removing a cluster node from the cluster configuration does not require cluster service downtime, unless the cluster service is running on the cluster node you would like to remove.

> Before you start the procedure of removing a cluster node from the cluster configuration, verify that no cluster resources and services are running on the node.

The steps required to successfully remove a cluster node from a running cluster configuration are as follows:

1. Stop the cluster software:
    - ○ Stop Ricci
    - ○ Stop RGmanager
    - ○ Stop CMAN

> Stop the cluster software on the cluster node you will remove from the cluster configuration.

2. Edit the CMAN configuration file:
    - ○ Remove the cluster node from the `<clusternodes>` section
    - ○ Remove the cluster node from the `<failoverdomains>` section, if required
    - ○ Increase the `config_version` parameter number

> Do not edit the CMAN `cluster.conf` configuration file on the cluster node you are going to remove from the cluster. Edit the CMAN configuration file on one of cluster nodes that will stay active.
>
> You can download an example CMAN `cluster.conf` configuration file from the `cman-conf-3.txt` file in the code bundle.

   - ○ Now the `config_version` parameter has been increased and the **node-4** cluster node has been removed from the `<clusternodes>` and `<failoverdomains>` sections

3. Distribute the CMAN configuration file:

   ° Validate the cluster configuration and distribute the CMAN configuration file to other, still active cluster nodes. In the following screenshot, you can see the command used to verify the cluster configuration and distribute the cluster.conf configuration file to other cluster nodes:

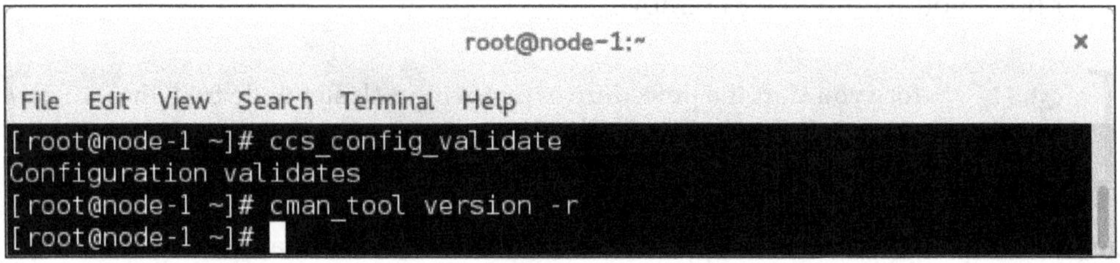

```
root@node-1:~                                          ×

File   Edit   View   Search   Terminal   Help
[root@node-1 ~]# ccs_config_validate
Configuration validates
[root@node-1 ~]# cman_tool version -r
[root@node-1 ~]#
```

4. Check the **Cluster Status** parameter to confirm that the cluster node was removed from the cluster configuration. In the following screenshot, you can see that the **node-4** cluster node has been successfully removed from the cluster:

```
root@node-1:~                                          ×

File   Edit   View   Search   Terminal   Help
[root@node-1 ~]# clustat
Cluster Status for hacluster @ Fri Mar  6 21:03:15 2015
Member Status: Quorate

 Member Name                           ID   Status
 ------ ----                           ---- ------
 node-1                                 1 Online, Local, rgmanager
 node-2                                 2 Online, rgmanager
 node-3                                 3 Online, rgmanager

 Service Name             Owner (Last)              State
 ------- ----             ----- ------              -----
 service:webserver        node-2                    started
[root@node-1 ~]#
```

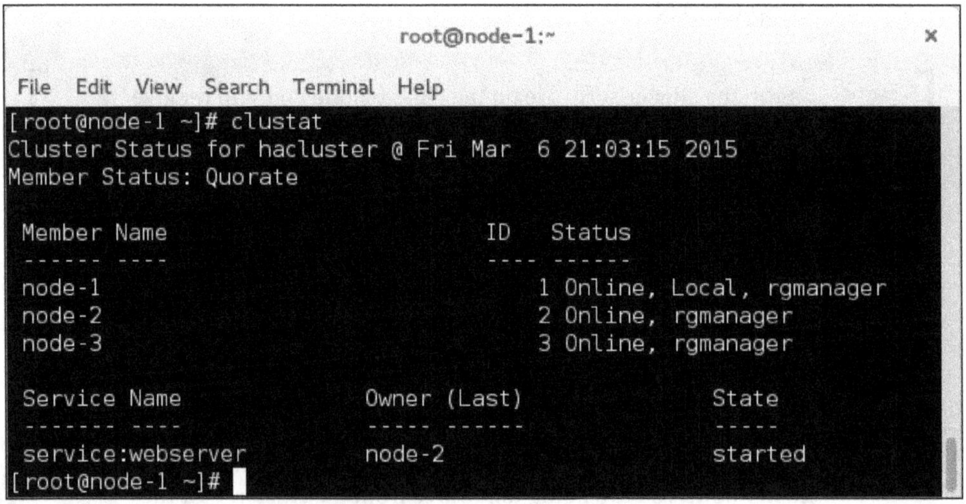

   ° The **node-4** cluster node is no longer listed and has been successfully removed from the cluster configuration

Summary

In this chapter, you learned how to add a cluster node to a running cluster configuration, and how to remove a cluster node from it without any cluster service disruption or downtime. In the following chapter, you will explore the cluster node fencing mechanism and how to configure cluster node fencing.

6
Fencing on CentOS 6

In this chapter, you will learn how to configure and test cluster node fencing on CentOS 6 with CMAN. You will familiarize yourself with the fencing options available and learn the syntax used to configure fencing. You will also learn how to take your fencing configuration for a test drive and make sure it is working as expected.

Fencing

Fencing is an important cluster task. It isolates a computer's cluster node when the node misbehaves, in order to protect the shared cluster resources and prevent cluster disruption. Fencing should not be used in a two-node cluster configuration because the nodes may go on a killing spree and kill each other. To work around this issue, you should implement a Quorum disk, as explained in *Chapter 8, Two-node Cluster Considerations on CentOS 6*. If you do not configure fencing, a misbehaving computer cluster node can corrupt the cluster data. This is why it is necessary to exclude the problematic cluster node from cluster configuration immediately. The name of the daemon running all fencing actions is **fenced**.

STONITH is a fencing technique that stands for **Shoot The Other Node In The Head**. STONITH fences a failed cluster node by rebooting or turning it off.

The following fencing devices are most commonly used in cluster environments:

- **APC switch**: APC switch is a rack mount automatic transfer switch that provides power for servers. APC switch has built-in network connectivity and enables remote management, which provides the ability to cut off the power if required.

- **IPMI Management Board**: IPMI is short for **Intelligent Platform Management Interface**. An IPMI is embedded on a server but completely independent from the server's system. It enables server monitoring and management even if the server is powered off.

- **HP Integrated Lights-Out (iLO) management board**: HP Integrated Lights-Out is also an embedded server management technology by Hewlett Packard. HP iLO is similar to IPMI and also allows administrators to turn a server on and off remotely.

- **Additional devices**: There are many additional fencing devices that can be used. A popular server manufacturer, DELL, also implements a similar **Dell Remote Access Controller (DRAC)** mechanism to support fencing. The fencing agents are provided by the `fence-agents` and `fence-virt` RPM packages, and the fencing scripts are located in the `/usr/sbin` folder. As an example, if you are running your cluster in a VMware-virtualized environment, you can use the `fence_vmware` fencing agent. It connects to ESX via SSH and powers off the problematic cluster node.

Fencing configuration

Fencing is configured in the CMAN configuration file, `/etc/cluster/cluster.conf`. It is defined by the `<fencedevides>` tag and must be placed after the `<clusternodes>` tag and before the `<rm>` tag in the CMAN configuration file. Within the `<fencedevices>` tag, different fence devices can be configured. There are different fence device options to be used with different fence devices.

The syntax for configuring a fence device is as follows:

```
<fencedevices>
  <fencedevice fencedevice_options/>
</fencedevices>
```

> More than one fence device can be configured simultaneously in the `/etc/cluster/cluster.conf` CMAN configuration file.

Once you have configured a fencing device, you need to configure the fencing method for each existing cluster node. The fence method configuration provides information on how to fence a specific cluster node.

The information provided varies, depending on the fencing device configured. If you are configuring the APC switch fencing, the fence method provides information about the power port the cluster node is connected to. If you are using the HP iLO option, the fence method provides the HP iLO IP address of the specific cluster node.

The syntax for configuring a cluster node fencing method is as follows:

```
<clusternode clusternode_options>
  <fence>
    <method method_options>
      <device fence_options/>
    </method>
  </fence>
</clusternode>
```

 More than one fence method can be configured simultaneously in the `/etc/cluster/cluster.conf` CMAN configuration file.

APC switch fencing

If you want to configure APC switch fencing, you must know the following information:

- **APC switch IP address**: The IP address of your APC switch
- **APC switch login details**: The username and password to use to successfully connect to the APC switch
- **APC switch port connections**: The power port numbers to which specific cluster nodes are connected

The syntax for configuring the APC switch fencing device is as follows:

```
<fencedevices>
  <fencedevice agent="fence_apc" ipaddr="192.168.88.100"
  login="apcuser" name="apcfence" passwd="apcpass"/>
</fencedevices>
```

- `agent="fence_apc"`: This option tells the fencing mechanism to use the existing `fence_apc` agent for fencing
- `ipaddr="192.168.88.100"`: This option is the IP address of the APC switch we want to connect to
- `login="apcuser"`: This is the username used when connecting to the APC switch
- `name="apcfence"`: This is a unique fence device name
- `passwd="apcpass"`: This is the password used when connecting to the APC switch

Additionally, you must configure fencing methods for your cluster nodes, as follows:

```
<clusternode clusternode_options>
  <fence>
    <method name="1">
      <device name="apcfence" port="1"/>
    </method>
  </fence>
</clusternode>
```

- name="1": This is a unique name of the fencing method
- name="apcfence": This is the name of the configured fence device to use
- port="1": This option tells the fence device to manage power port 1 on the APC switch

The full CMAN configuration file, with APC switch fencing configured, can be downloaded from the `cman-conf-1.txt` file from the code bundle.

IPMI management board fencing

To configure your cluster with IPMI management board fencing, you should know the following information:

- **IPMI IP address of each cluster node**: This is the IP address of the IPMI management board. Each cluster node has its own IPMI IP address.

- **IPMI login details for each cluster node**: These are the username and password to use to successfully connect to the cluster node IPMI management board. Each cluster node can have different IPMI login details.

The syntax for configuring the IPMI management board fencing device is as follows:

```
<fencedevices>
  <fencedevice agent="fence_ipmilan" ipaddr="192.168.88.100"
  login="ipmiuser1" name="impifence1" passwd="ipmipass1"/>

  <fencedevice agent="fence_ipmilan" ipaddr="192.168.88.101"
  login="ipmiuser2" name="impifence2" passwd="ipmipass2"/>

  <fencedevice agent="fence_ipmilan" ipaddr="192.168.88.102"
  login="ipmiuser3" name="impifence3" passwd="ipmipass3"/>
</fencedevices>
```

- `agent="fence_ipmilan"`: This option tells the fencing mechanism to use the existing `fence_ipmilan` agent for fencing.
- `ipaddr="192.168.88.100"`: This option is the IP address of the IPMI management board of the first cluster node. Each cluster node has a different IPMI IP address to connect to.
- `login="ipmiuser1"`: This is the username used to connect to the IPMI management board on the first cluster node. Each cluster node uses a different IPMI login username.
- `name="ipmifence1"`: This is a unique fence device name for the first cluster node. Each cluster node fence device has a different name.
- `passwd="ipmipass1"`: This is the password used when connecting to the IPMI management board of the first cluster node. Each cluster node uses a different IPMI password to connect.

Additionally, you must configure the fencing methods for your cluster nodes, as follows:

```
<clusternode clusternode_options>
  <fence>
    <method name="1">
      <device name="ipmifence1"/>
    </method>
  </fence>
</clusternode>
```

- `name="1"`: This is the unique name of the fencing method
- `name="ipmifence1"`: This is the name of the configured fence device to use

The full CMAN configuration file, with IPMI management board fencing configured, can be downloaded from the `cman-conf-2.txt` file in the code bundle.

HP iLO management board fencing

To configure the cluster with HP iLO management board fencing, you should know the following information:

- **HP iLO address of each cluster node**: This is the IP address of the HP iLO management board. Each cluster node has its own HP iLO IP address.

- **HP iLO login details for each cluster node**: These are the username and password to use to successfully connect to the cluster node HP iLO management board. Each cluster node can have different HP iLO login details.

The syntax for configuring the HP iLO management board fencing device is as follows:

```
<fencedevices>
  <fencedevice agent="fence_ilo" ipaddr="192.168.88.100"
  login="hpilouser1" name="hpilofence1" passwd="hpilopass1"/>
  <fencedevice agent="fence_ilo" ipaddr="192.168.88.101"
  login="hpilouser2" name="hpilofence2" passwd="hpilopass2"/>
  <fencedevice agent="fence_ilo" ipaddr="192.168.88.102"
  login="hpilouser3" name="hpilofence3" passwd="hpilopass3"/>
</fencedevices>
```

- `agent="fence_ilo"`: This option tells the fencing mechanism to use the existing `fence_ilo` agent for fencing.
- `ipaddr="192.168.88.100"`: This option is the IP address of the HP iLO management board of the first cluster node. Each cluster node has a different HP iLO IP address to connect to.
- `login="hpilouser1"`: This is the username used to connect to the HP iLO management board on the first cluster node. Each cluster node uses a different HP iLO login username.
- `name="hpilofence1"`: This is a unique fence device name for the first cluster node. Each cluster node fence device has a different name.
- `passwd="hpilopass1"`: This is the password used when connecting to the HP iLO management board of the first cluster node. Each cluster node uses a different HP iLO password to connect.

Additionally, you must configure the fencing methods for your cluster nodes, like this:

```
<clusternode clusternode_options>
  <fence>
    <method name="1">
      <device name="hpilofence1"/>
    </method>
  </fence>
</clusternode>
```

- `name="1"`: This is a unique name of the fencing method
- `name="hpilofence1"`: This is the name of the configured fence device to use

The full CMAN configuration file, with HP iLO management board fencing configured, can be downloaded from the `cman-conf-3.txt` file in the code bundle.

As you can see, the IPMI and HP iLO management board fencing configurations are very similar, as both management boards work on the same principle. Both of them are embedded in the server and have network connectivity, which enables authentication and remote server management.

Fencing test

When you configure a task as important as fencing, it is necessary to test it to make sure it works as expected. Luckily, the developers of such cluster software are also aware of this fact, and you can easily manage and test the fencing configuration with the `fence_check`, `fence_tool`, and `fence_node` commands.

- `fence_check`: This command is used to check the fencing configuration in the CMAN configuration file. The `fence_check` command checks whether the configured fence devices and cluster node fencing methods used are valid or not, and provides a verbose output.
- `fence_tool`: The `fence_tool` command can be used to print information about the fence domain and also remove or join the cluster node from or to the fence domain.
- `fence_node`: The `fence_node` command is used to manually test the fencing. You can use this command to manually fence the node you want.

The `fenced` fencing daemon also provides a log file where you can get all of the information about fencing daemon and fencing actions. The `fenced` daemon log file is placed at `/var/log/cluster/fenced.log`.

Fence master node

Before you can start testing the fencing configuration with the `fence_check` command, you must find out which cluster node is currently the fence domain master node.

This can be easily achieved with the `fence_tool ls` command, which prints information about the fence domain. In the following screenshot, you can see the `fence_tool` command being run on the **node-2** cluster node — the current fence master — used to view the current fencing configuration status:

```
root@node-2:~                                            ×

File   Edit   View   Search   Terminal   Help
[root@node-2 ~]# fence_tool ls
fence domain
member count  3
victim count  0
victim now    0
master nodeid 2
wait state    none
members       1 2 3

[root@node-2 ~]#
```

Here, you can also see that there are currently three cluster nodes with configured fencing methods. The `victim count` parameter is `0`, which means that no cluster nodes have been fenced yet. The information we currently require is the `master nodeid` parameter information, which tells us that the fence master node is the cluster node with node ID equal to `2`.

In order to successfully perform the `fence_check` configuration check, you must run it on the cluster node with node ID equal to `2`.

Fence check

You must run the `fence_check` command to see whether the fencing configuration you provided in the CMAN configuration file turns out to be valid. The `fence_check` command must be run on the current fence master node, and it provides a verbose output. In the following screenshot, you can see the `fence_check` command output, running on the fence master **node-2** cluster node:

```
root@node-2:~                                            ×

File   Edit   View   Search   Terminal   Help
[root@node-2 ~]# fence_check
fence_check run at Thu Mar 12 21:05:32 CET 2015 pid: 16461
Testing node-1 method 1: success
Testing node-2 method 1: success
Testing node-3 method 1: success
[root@node-2 ~]#
```

In this screenshot, our fencing configuration is checked and appears to be valid. If your `fence_check` command fails, be sure to recheck the CMAN configuration file for errors. Only once your fencing configuration validates will you be able to proceed to the next step.

Fence node

Once you have successfully completed the `fence_check` command step, you can proceed to the next step—manually test-fencing a cluster node. The syntax to manually fence the cluster node with the `fence_node` tool is simple:

```
fence_node nodename
```

By running the `fence_node nodename` command, the specific cluster node will be powered off or rebooted, depending on the default action used by the fencing agent.

For the `fence_node` command test, we can refer to the cluster status screenshot before the `fence_node` command and a screenshot of the cluster status after the `fence_node` command.

In this screenshot, you can see the cluster status before running the `fence_node` command:

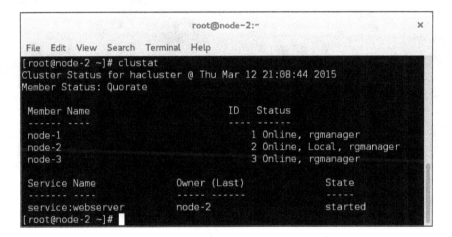

You can continue by running the fence_node node-3 command. In the following screenshot, you can see the fence_node node-3 command issued on the **node-2** cluster node:

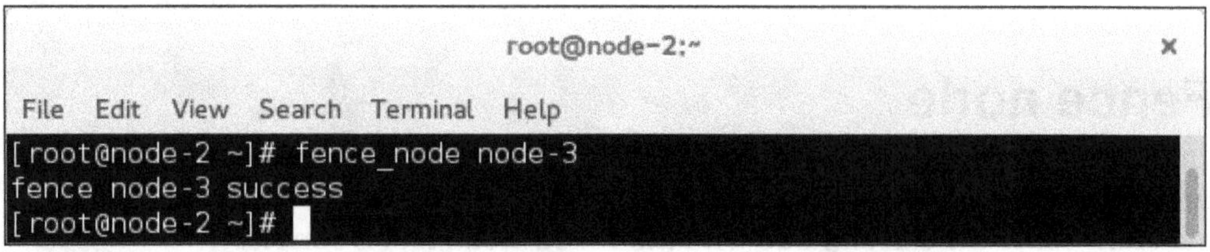

```
                              root@node-2:~                              ×

 File   Edit   View   Search   Terminal   Help
[root@node-2 ~]# fence_node node-3
fence node-3 success
[root@node-2 ~]#
```

You can see that the fence_node node-3 command was executed successfully.

The cluster status upon fencing the cluster node called **node-3** is as shown in this screenshot:

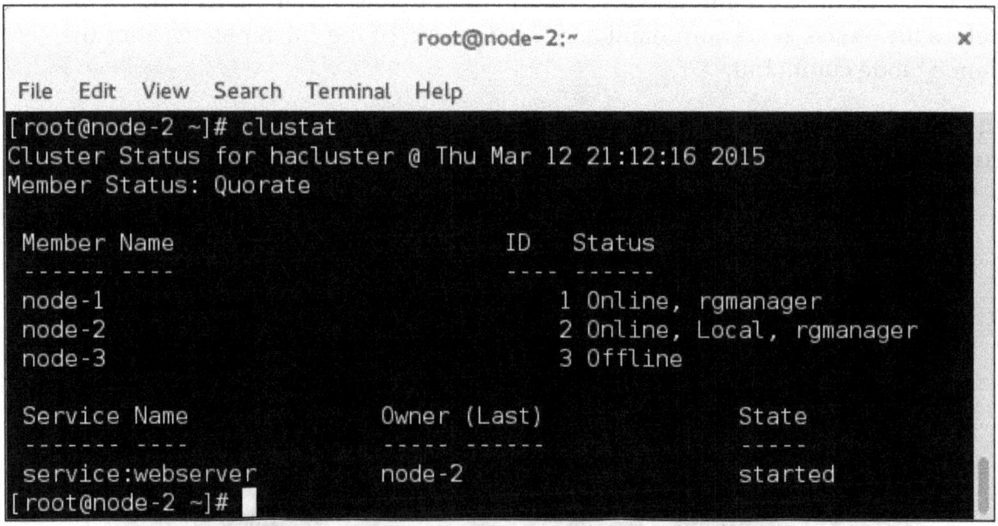

```
                              root@node-2:~                              ×

 File   Edit   View   Search   Terminal   Help
[root@node-2 ~]# clustat
Cluster Status for hacluster @ Thu Mar 12 21:12:16 2015
Member Status: Quorate

 Member Name                          ID   Status
 ------ ----                          ---- ------
 node-1                                1 Online, rgmanager
 node-2                                2 Online, Local, rgmanager
 node-3                                3 Offline

 Service Name              Owner (Last)                    State
 ------- ----              ----- ------                    -----
 service:webserver         node-2                          started
[root@node-2 ~]#
```

You can see that the cluster node called **node-3** is offline due to the executed fencing command.

You should repeat the fencing test process for every cluster node, preferably as many times as possible, just to make sure that, when an actual problem in the cluster occurs, the fencing mechanism is reliable.

Summary

In this chapter, you learned what fencing is all about. You learned about the fence devices you can use and how they must be configured. Since a fencing mechanism is an important cluster task that needs to be tested thoroughly, you were also provided with information on how to test your fencing configuration and manually fence a cluster node for testing purposes. In the next chapter, you will see how to run cluster failover tests for different scenarios.

Testing Failover on CentOS 6

In previous chapters, you learned how to install and configure a cluster software stack on CentOS 6, and also how to configure and manage cluster nodes and cluster resources. In this chapter, you will test the cluster configuration by manually triggering cluster node failure and making sure that the migration of configured resources to an existing, healthy node is successful.

Note that you should run as many tests as possible with different sorts of scenarios before deploying your cluster on the production environment. In this way, you can make sure that the cluster configuration is correct and avoid cluster service downtime.

Hardware failure

If your cluster node experiences a CPU, RAM, or motherboard failure, it is an unrecoverable failure and the cluster node will go offline. The cluster fencing mechanism will try to fence the problematic cluster node anyway, making sure it is not accessing the cluster's shared storage, which could lead to cluster data corruption. If your cluster node experiences disk failure, it should not affect the cluster node operation due to RAID disk redundancy, which enables normal cluster operation.

The cluster from the following example is configured to provide a **webserver** cluster service that includes a cluster IP address and an Apache **webserver** instance. The **webserver** cluster service is running on the **node-1** cluster node. In the following screenshot, you can see the current state of the cluster:

```
                                    root@node-2:~                                    ×

 File  Edit  View  Search  Terminal  Help
[root@node-2 ~]# clustat
Cluster Status for hacluster @ Wed Feb 25 21:44:35 2015
Member Status: Quorate

Member Name                              ID   Status
------ ----                              ---- ------
  node-1                                   1 Online, rgmanager
  node-2                                   2 Online, Local, rgmanager
  node-3                                   3 Online, rgmanager

Service Name                Owner (Last)                      State
------- ----                ----- ------                      -----
  service:webserver         node-1                            started
[root@node-2 ~]#
```

You can proceed to simulate hardware failure on the part of the **node-1** cluster node. This can be done by cutting off the power to the cluster node.

Once the cluster node is powered off, check the cluster status to see whether the **webserver** service was successfully migrated to an operational cluster node, and is up-and-running. In this screenshot, you can see the cluster status after simulating the **node-1** cluster node failure:

```
                                    root@node-2:~                                    ×

 File  Edit  View  Search  Terminal  Help
[root@node-2 ~]# clustat
Cluster Status for hacluster @ Wed Feb 25 21:45:04 2015
Member Status: Quorate

Member Name                              ID   Status
------ ----                              ---- ------
  node-1                                   1 Offline
  node-2                                   2 Online, Local, rgmanager
  node-3                                   3 Online, rgmanager

Service Name                Owner (Last)                      State
------- ----                ----- ------                      -----
  service:webserver         node-3                            started
[root@node-2 ~]#
```

As you can see, the **node-1** cluster node status is offline, and the **webserver** service was successfully migrated and started on an operational **node-3** cluster node. You can consider the hardware failure test successful.

Network failure

In the following example, you will perform a cluster node network failure test. Network failure can occur due to network infrastructure equipment failure or cluster node network card failure. An important part of this test is the fact that the problematic cluster node with the network failure could still be online and could still have access to the shared cluster storage and cluster data. It is very important for the fencing mechanism to fence the problematic cluster node and make sure it is offline, without access to the cluster data.

The cluster from the following example is configured to provide a **webserver** cluster service. The **webserver** cluster service is a combination of a cluster IP address and an Apache webserver instance. The **webserver** cluster service is running on the **node-3** cluster node. In the following screenshot, you can see the cluster status prior to the network failure test:

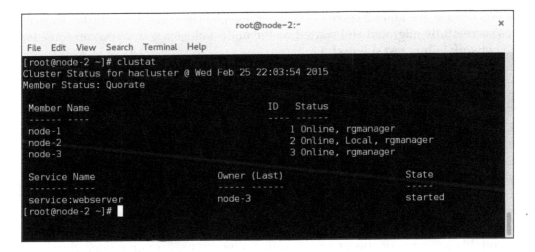

You can proceed to simulate the **node-3** cluster node's network failure by removing the connected network cables from the network card on the **node-3** cluster node. Then observe the cluster failover process.

Once you have successfully removed the network cables from the network cards, check the cluster status to verify that the **webserver** service was successfully migrated to one of the operational cluster nodes. In the following screenshot, you can see the cluster status after simulating the **node-3** cluster node's network failure:

```
                                    root@node-2:~                                ×

 File   Edit   View   Search   Terminal   Help
[root@node-2 ~]# clustat
Cluster Status for hacluster @ Wed Feb 25 22:04:23 2015
Member Status: Quorate

 Member Name                              ID   Status
 ------ ----                              ---- ------
 node-1                                    1 Online, rgmanager
 node-2                                    2 Online, Local, rgmanager
 node-3                                    3 Offline

 Service Name                 Owner (Last)                       State
 ------- ----                 ----- ------                       -----
 service:webserver            node-1                             started
[root@node-2 ~]# 
```

As you can see, the **node-3** cluster node is offline and the **webserver** cluster service was successfully migrated and started on the **node-1** cluster node. You can consider the network failure test successful.

Summary

In this chapter, you learned that testing your cluster configuration is very important before deploying your cluster on the production environment. You saw how to test for hardware and network failure, and how to check whether the test was successful or not. You should think of additional cluster failover tests to perform, in order to cover as many scenarios as possible. The failover tests depend on the cluster infrastructure and cluster configuration, and are specific to each cluster. The cluster administrator should have an idea of which tests they should perform. By thoroughly testing your cluster configuration, you can prevent unwanted cluster service downtime. In the next chapter, you will familiarize yourself with two-node cluster considerations on CentOS 6. You will learn how to configure the cluster for two-node operation and also how to add a Quorum disk to a cluster configuration.

8

Two-node Cluster
Considerations on CentOS 6

In previous chapters, you learned what high availability is all about and how to achieve it. You also learned how to install and configure a three-node cluster on CentOS 6. A guide to high availability on CentOS 6 cannot be complete without mentioning considerations for a two-node cluster configuration. In this chapter, you will learn the downsides of using a two-node cluster configuration and workarounds to resolve the issues.

Quorum in a two-node cluster

You learned about quorum in *Chapter 2, Meet the Cluster Stack on CentOS*. Quorum is the minimum number of cluster member votes required to perform a cluster operation. Without quorum, the cluster cannot operate. Quorum is achieved when the majority of cluster members vote to execute a specific cluster operation. If the majority of the cluster members do not vote, the cluster operation will not be performed.

You've probably understood where this is going. In a two-node cluster configuration, the maximum number of expected votes is two—each cluster node has one vote. In a cluster node failure scenario, only one cluster node is active and it has only one vote. In such a configuration, quorum cannot be reached, since a majority of the votes cannot be delivered. The single cluster node is stuck at 50 percent and will never get past it. Therefore, the cluster will never operate normally this way. Luckily, there are solutions to work around this problem. The first solution is to reconfigure the cluster to be quorate with only one active cluster node. The second solution implements a quorum disk to resolve the cluster quorum by adding another vote to the cluster. For normal two-node cluster operation, you should implement one of the two possible solutions. The quorum provider in the CentOS 6 cluster stack is CMAN.

Two-node cluster configuration

As I said, the first option is to reconfigure your cluster to be quorate with only one active cluster node. To do so, you must edit the `cluster.conf` configuration file and tell the cluster that you are running a two-node cluster configuration and the number of expected votes to reach quorum is 1. You can achieve this by executing the following line:

```
<cman two_node="1" expected_votes="1"/>
```

- `two_node="1"`: This parameter tells the cluster that it is running a two-node cluster configuration
- `expected_votes="1"`: This parameter is the number of votes expected for the cluster to be quorate

You can download an example two-node `cluster.conf` configuration file from the `cman-conf-2.txt` file from the code bundle.

You must always disable fencing in a two-node cluster configuration without a quorum disk in order to avoid fence race scenarios, where the two cluster nodes kill each other.

Quorum disk

The second solution to the quorum problem in a two-node cluster configuration is to implement an additional quorum disk. A quorum disk is a shared storage block device both cluster nodes have access to. The Cluster and cluster nodes use this disk as cluster configuration storage and also as a secondary heartbeat communication channel. A quorum disk brings another vote to the cluster configuration, therefore eliminating the problem of a two-node cluster configuration quorum. A quorum disk can also be used as a secondary cluster heartbeat communication channel, and can therefore resolve cluster split-brain situations in the case of network communication failure.

With the quorum disk implemented, in the event of a cluster node failure quorum is reached by one cluster node vote and one quorum disk vote, and the cluster can continue to perform its normal operation.

The quorum disk solution is not reserved specifically for a two-node cluster configuration. It can be used as an additional quorum and heartbeat mechanism in multinode cluster configurations as well.

The following steps must be performed to successfully implement a quorum disk solution on your CentOS 6 cluster:

1. **Shared storage**: To successfully implement a quorum disk, you must provide a shared storage solution for your cluster nodes: Fiber Channel, iSCSI, or some other array storage. All cluster nodes must have access to the same block device. The minimum size of a block device is 10 MB, and the size should not be more than 1 GB.

2. **Initialize the Quorum disk**: Create a new partition on the shared block device, and initialize the quorum partition using the `mkqdisk` command. The syntax is as follows:

    ```
    mkqdisk -c <device> -1 <label>
    ```

    - `<device>`: This parameter is the partition you would like to use for quorum.
    - `<label>`: This parameter is the unique name you would like to assign to the quorum disk. The label will be referenced in the `cluster.conf` file.

    Once the command is initialized, you can check the status of the quorum partition with the `mkqdisk -L` command.

3. **Edit the cluster.conf configuration file**: You must edit the `cluster.conf` configuration file and add the quorum disk configuration. The following lines configure a quorum disk in a two-node cluster configuration:

    ```
    <quorumd interval="3" tko="10" label="qdisk" votes="1"/>
    <cman deadnode_timeout="100"  expected_votes="2"/>
    ```

    - `interval="3"`: This parameter is the frequency of read/write cycles on the quorum disk
    - `tko="10"`: This parameter is the number of cycles the node must miss in order to be declared dead
    - `label="qdisk"`: This parameter is the unique name of the quorum disk
    - `deadnode_timeout="100"`: This parameter is the number of seconds to wait before removing a node from the cluster configuration
    - `expected_voter="2"`: This parameter is the number of votes expected for the cluster to be quorate

You can download an example two-node `cluster.conf` configuration file from the `cman-conf-1.txt` file from the code bundle.

4. **Validate and distribute the cluster configuration**: Once you are done with the preceding steps, you can validate your cluster configuration and distribute it to the other cluster nodes.

Summary

You have successfully finished the chapters on CentOS 6 cluster installation and configuration. You learned how to prepare the operating system for cluster software; install, configure, and test cluster software; manage cluster resources and cluster nodes; and configure fencing and quorum disk. You should now be able to fully and individually administer a CentOS 6 cluster running on Corosync, CMAN, and RGManager.

9
Cluster Stack Software
on CentOS 7

Installing cluster stack software on CentOS version 7 is preferable. The cluster stack software on CentOS 7 uses more recent packages with longer life compared to the cluster stack on CentOS version 6, and also provides more features and flexibility. The official Red Hat Enterprise Linux 7 cluster suite is the cluster messaging layer provided by Corosync 2.x, and the cluster resource manager layer provided by Pacemaker. CentOS version 7 and Red Hat Enterprise Linux 7 provide the same cluster stack software.

Cluster infrastructure

In the upcoming chapters, you will be presented with a practical example of cluster installation and configuration. The three-node cluster used in the following example runs in a virtual environment. All virtual cluster nodes run on CentOS version 7. A 64-bit minimal installation is used to build the cluster. SELinux and IPTables are enabled and run on all cluster nodes. The virtual machines have exactly the same resource specifications, as follows:

- A CPU core
- 768 MB RAM
- A 10 GB disk
- A 1 GB disk
- Two network adapters

- The following are the cluster nodes' fully qualified domain names:
    - ° node-1.geekpeek.net (short name: node-1)
    - ° node-2.geekpeek.net (short name: node-2)
    - ° node-3.geekpeek.net (short name: node-3)

Due to my virtualized environment limitations, the network IP addresses of both cluster node network interfaces are in the same network subnet—192.168.88.0/24.

The assigned static cluster node IP addresses are as follows:

- 192.168.88.10, 192.168.88.11: node-1.geekpeek.net
- 192.168.88.20, 192.168.88.21: node-2.geekpeek.net
- 192.168.88.30, 192.168.88.31: node-3.geekpeek.net

It is preferred to have a separate network subnet for cluster communication and for all other kinds of traffic. For production environments, each cluster node should have at least two network interfaces. The cluster node messaging traffic should be separated from all other kinds of traffic. This is usually done with a different network subnet configuration.

Cluster operating system preparation

I assume your cluster nodes are all set up; power, network, and other cables are connected; the operating system is installed; and disks are partitioned the way you want them. Before you can start with the cluster stack software installation and configuration, you must carefully follow the steps in the upcoming sections.

Network configuration

You must configure a static IP address for all available network interfaces on all cluster nodes. You can do this by editing the /etc/sysconfig/network-scripts/ifcfg-enpXsY files.

In the following screenshot, you can see the network interface configuration for the **node-1** cluster node:

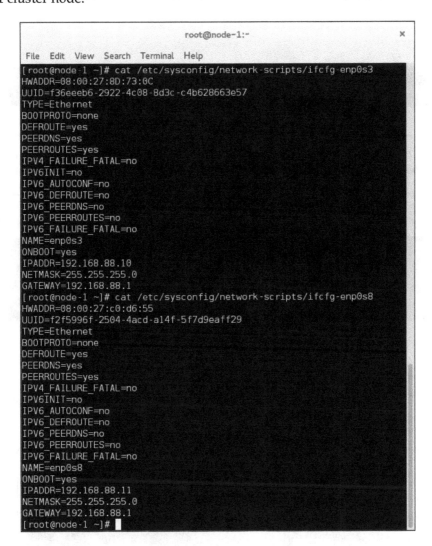

 Change the **BOOTPROTO** line to **none**. This specifies that no boot protocol is used for this interface, since this interface has a static IP address.

Add the **IPADDR, NETMASK,** and **GATEWAY** lines according to your environment and networking configuration.

You can completely remove the **NetworkManager** service. In this screenshot, you can see the command used to remove the **NetworkManager** service from the system:

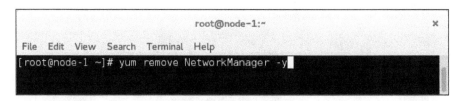

Alternatively, you can stop and disable the **NetworkManager** service entirely without removing it. In the following screenshot, you can see the commands used to stop the **NetworkManager** service and disable **NetworkManager** from starting at boot:

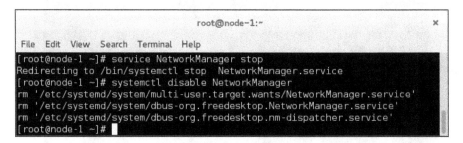

 You must remove or disable the **NetworkManager** service because you will want to avoid any automated configuration of network interfaces on your cluster nodes.

After removing or disabling the **NetworkManager** service, you must restart the networking service.

In this screenshot, you can see the command used to restart the network service:

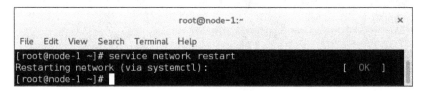

 You must reconfigure the network interfaces and restart the networking service on all cluster nodes. Also do not forget to remove, or stop and disable, the **NetworkManager** service.

NTP configuration

You must install and start the NTP time synchronization service to maintain consistent time throughout the cluster. In the following screenshot, you can see the command used to install the NTP time synchronization service:

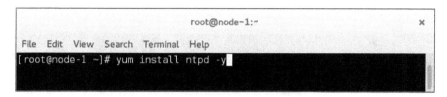

 By default, the NTP installation time is synchronized with the official CentOS NTP servers. If you want to change this, edit the NTP configuration file at /etc/ntp.conf.

Start the NTP service and make sure it starts at boot. In this screenshot, you can see the commands used to start the ntpd service and make it start at boot time:

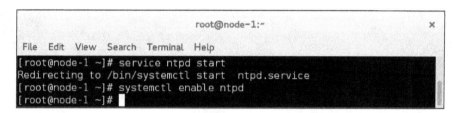

 You must install and start the NTP service on all cluster nodes. Also do not forget to make it start at boot.

DNS configuration

You must configure the domain name servers, fully qualified domain names, and the hosts file. The domain name service is provided by the DNS servers that are configured in the /etc/resolv.conf file. It is recommended you configure at least two DNS servers; add more if you like.

You must edit the `/etc/resolv.conf` file and insert the IP addresses of your DNS servers. In the following screenshot, you can see the DNS configuration on the **node-1** cluster node:

```
                              root@node-1:~                          ×
 File  Edit  View  Search  Terminal  Help
[root@node-1 ~]# cat /etc/resolv.conf
nameserver 192.168.88.1
nameserver 192.168.88.2
[root@node-1 ~]#
```

You must also configure the **Fully Qualified Domain Names (FQDN)** for the cluster nodes by editing the `/etc/hostname` file and inserting the FQDN of your cluster node. In this screenshot, you can see the FQDN configuration of the **node-1** cluster node:

```
                              root@node-1:~                          ×
 File  Edit  View  Search  Terminal  Help
[root@node-1 ~]# cat /etc/hostname
node-1.geekpeek.net
[root@node-1 ~]#
```

 Note that cluster node reboot is required for hostname changes to take effect.

Edit the `/etc/hosts` file and add the IP address, followed by an FQDN and a short cluster node name for every available cluster node network interface. In the following screenshot, you can see the hosts file configuration for the **node-1** cluster node:

```
                              root@node-1:~                          ×
 File  Edit  View  Search  Terminal  Help
[root@node-1 ~]# cat /etc/hosts
127.0.0.1    localhost localhost.localdomain localhost4 localhost4.localdomain4
::1          localhost localhost.localdomain localhost6 localhost6.localdomain6
192.168.88.10 node-1.geekpeek.net node-1
192.168.88.11 node-1.geekpeek.net node-1
192.168.88.20 node-2.geekpeek.net node-2
192.168.88.21 node-2.geekpeek.net node-2
192.168.88.30 node-3.geekpeek.net node-3
192.168.88.31 node-3.geekpeek.net node-3
[root@node-1 ~]#
```

You must configure the DNS servers and fully qualified domain names in the `/etc/hosts` file on all cluster nodes.

To finish, you must check and confirm connectivity among the cluster nodes. You can do this by simply releasing a `ping` command to every cluster node. In this screenshot, you can see the `ping` test performed from the cluster node:

```
root@node-1:~                                          ×
File   Edit   View   Search   Terminal   Help
[root@node-1 ~]# ping -c 1 node-2
PING node-2.geekpeek.net (192.168.88.20) 56(84) bytes of data.
64 bytes from node-2.geekpeek.net (192.168.88.20): icmp_seq=1 ttl=64 time=0.966
ms

--- node-2.geekpeek.net ping statistics ---
1 packets transmitted, 1 received, 0% packet loss, time 0ms
rtt min/avg/max/mdev = 0.966/0.966/0.966/0.000 ms
[root@node-1 ~]# ping -c 1 node-3
PING node-3.geekpeek.net (192.168.88.30) 56(84) bytes of data.
64 bytes from node-3.geekpeek.net (192.168.88.30): icmp_seq=1 ttl=64 time=0.249
ms

--- node-3.geekpeek.net ping statistics ---
1 packets transmitted, 1 received, 0% packet loss, time 0ms
rtt min/avg/max/mdev = 0.249/0.249/0.249/0.000 ms
[root@node-1 ~]# █
```

 You must check network connectivity among all the cluster nodes, and make sure that all **Internet Control Message Protocol (ICMP)** packets are transmitted and received and there is no packet loss.

Installing and configuring Corosync

Now let's get down to business. You must configure the firewalld daemon on your cluster nodes to allow cluster communication traffic among the cluster nodes. Add a firewall rule to allow UDP traffic on 5404 and 5405, and reload the firewalld daemon. In the following screenshot, you can see the commands used for firewalld daemon reconfiguration to allow Corosync traffic:

```
                        root@node-1:~                          ✕

 File   Edit   View   Search   Terminal   Help
[root@node-1 ~]# firewall-cmd --permanent --add-port=5404/udp
success
[root@node-1 ~]# firewall-cmd --permanent --add-port=5405/udp
success
[root@node-1 ~]# firewall-cmd --reload
success
[root@node-1 ~]# █
```

 The default Corosync cluster communication ports are 5404 and 5405, on which the UDP protocol is used. The ports are configured in the /etc/corosync/corosync.conf configuration file. If you want to change the default Corosync communication ports, be sure to change the IPTables accordingly.

Install Corosync and make sure it is started at boot. In this screenshot, you can see the commands used to install Corosync:

```
                        root@node-1:~                          ✕

 File   Edit   View   Search   Terminal   Help
[root@node-1 ~]# yum install corosync -y█
```

Here is a screenshot showing you how to make Corosync start at boot time:

```
                        root@node-1:~                          ✕

 File   Edit   View   Search   Terminal   Help
[root@node-1 ~]# systemctl enable corosync
[root@node-1 ~]# █
```

Note that you must allow Corosync traffic by adding the `firewalld` rules, reload the `firewalld` service, install Corosync, and make it start at boot on all the cluster nodes.

Generate the Corosync encryption keys with the `corosync-keygen` command. In this way, you can increase cluster security by encrypting cluster communication traffic. In the following screenshot, you can see the process of Corosync encryption key generation:

```
                              root@node-1:~                            ×

  File  Edit  View  Search  Terminal  Help
[root@node-1 ~]# corosync-keygen
Corosync Cluster Engine Authentication key generator.
Gathering 1024 bits for key from /dev/random.
Press keys on your keyboard to generate entropy.
Press keys on your keyboard to generate entropy (bits = 152).
Press keys on your keyboard to generate entropy (bits = 216).
Press keys on your keyboard to generate entropy (bits = 280).
Press keys on your keyboard to generate entropy (bits = 344).
Press keys on your keyboard to generate entropy (bits = 408).
Press keys on your keyboard to generate entropy (bits = 472).
Press keys on your keyboard to generate entropy (bits = 536).
Press keys on your keyboard to generate entropy (bits = 600).
Press keys on your keyboard to generate entropy (bits = 664).
Press keys on your keyboard to generate entropy (bits = 728).
Press keys on your keyboard to generate entropy (bits = 792).
Press keys on your keyboard to generate entropy (bits = 856).
Press keys on your keyboard to generate entropy (bits = 920).
Press keys on your keyboard to generate entropy (bits = 984).
Writing corosync key to /etc/corosync/authkey.
[root@node-1 ~]#
```

 If you want to speed up the key generation process, you can use the `dd if=/dev/urandom of=file.txt` command running in parallel with the `corosync-keygen` command. Stop the `dd` command when the key is generated and delete the generated file.

Create the Corosync configuration file by copying it from the sample configuration file. In this screenshot, you can see the copy command being used:

```
                              root@node-1:~                            ×

  File  Edit  View  Search  Terminal  Help
[root@node-1 ~]# cp /etc/corosync/corosync.conf.example /etc/corosync/corosync.conf
[root@node-1 ~]#
```

Edit the newly created Corosync configuration file and perform the following steps:

1. Uncomment the `provider: corosync_votequorum` instance in the `quorum` section.

2. Remove all the commented-out lines — lines starting with the # symbol.

3. Change the `crypto_cipher` parameter to `aes256`.

4. Change the `crypto_hash` parameter to `sha256`.

5. Change the `bindnetaddr` parameter to the current cluster node's IP address.

6. Change the `to_syslog` parameter to `no`. Add a `nodelist` section at the end of the configuration file that lists all three nodes.

You can download the full Corosync configuration example from the `corosync-conf-1.txt` file in the code bundle.

Let's take a look at the following terms:

- `crypto_cipher`: This parameter is used to encrypt cluster communication traffic and should be changed to `aes256`.

- `crypto_hash`: This parameter is used to encrypt cluster communication traffic and should be changed to `sha256`.

- `bindnetaddr`: Change this parameter to the IP address of the cluster node you are currently on and the network interface you would like to use for cluster communication.

- `to_syslog`: Change this parameter to `no` if you want to avoid double logging. The default Corosync configuration is in the `/var/log/messages` and `/var/log/cluster/corosync.log` log files.

- `quorum`: This section provides Quorum capabilities. The `provider` line should be set to `corosync_votequorum`.

- `nodelist`: This section provides information about the cluster nodes, their node IDs, and IP addresses.

Distribute the Corosync configuration file and the Corosync `authkey` file among the other cluster nodes. In the following screenshot, you can see the files being distributed from the **node-1** cluster node using the `scp` command. For this command to be available on your system, the `openssh-clients` package must be installed first.

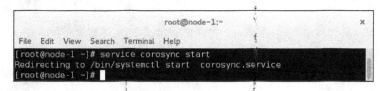

```
                          root@node-1:~                          ×

File   Edit   View   Search   Terminal   Help
[root@node-1 ~]# scp /etc/corosync/corosync.conf node-2:/etc/corosync/
corosync.conf                              100%   421     0.4KB/s   00:00
[root@node-1 ~]# scp /etc/corosync/corosync.conf node-3:/etc/corosync/
corosync.conf                              100%   421     0.4KB/s   00:00
[root@node-1 ~]# scp /etc/corosync/authkey node-2:/etc/corosync/
authkey                                    100%   128     0.1KB/s   00:00
[root@node-1 ~]# scp /etc/corosync/authkey node-3:/etc/corosync/
authkey                                    100%   128     0.1KB/s   00:00
[root@node-1 ~]# █
```

 Once the Corosync configuration file is transferred to other cluster nodes, you must change the `bindnetaddr` parameter to the IP address of the cluster node you are currently editing the `corosync.conf` configuration file on.

Start the Corosync service. In this screenshot, you can see the command used to start the Corosync service on the **node-1** cluster node:

```
                          root@node-1:~                          ×

File   Edit   View   Search   Terminal   Help
[root@node-1 ~]# service corosync start
Redirecting to /bin/systemctl start  corosync.service
[root@node-1 ~]# █
```

 You must start the Corosync service on all the cluster nodes.

You can check the Corosync membership status using the `corosync-cmapctl` command. In the following screenshot, you can see the command used to check the membership status:

```
                          root@node-1:~                          ×

File   Edit   View   Search   Terminal   Help
[root@node-1 ~]# corosync-cmapctl |grep members
runtime.totem.pg.mrp.srp.members.1.config_version (u64) = 0
runtime.totem.pg.mrp.srp.members.1.ip (str) = r(0) ip(192.168.88.10)
runtime.totem.pg.mrp.srp.members.1.join_count (u32) = 1
runtime.totem.pg.mrp.srp.members.1.status (str) = joined
runtime.totem.pg.mrp.srp.members.2.config_version (u64) = 0
runtime.totem.pg.mrp.srp.members.2.ip (str) = r(0) ip(192.168.88.20)
runtime.totem.pg.mrp.srp.members.2.join_count (u32) = 1
runtime.totem.pg.mrp.srp.members.2.status (str) = joined
runtime.totem.pg.mrp.srp.members.3.config_version (u64) = 0
runtime.totem.pg.mrp.srp.members.3.ip (str) = r(0) ip(192.168.88.30)
runtime.totem.pg.mrp.srp.members.3.join_count (u32) = 1
runtime.totem.pg.mrp.srp.members.3.status (str) = joined
[root@node-1 ~]# █
```

You can use the grep command to search for the members string in the corosync-objctl command output to get the information you need. As you can see in the preceding screenshot, the IP addresses of all three cluster nodes should be listed. This means that all three cluster nodes have successfully joined the cluster.

Continue to check the cluster's Quorum status using the corosync-quorumtool command.

In this screenshot, you can see the command used to check the cluster's Quorum status:

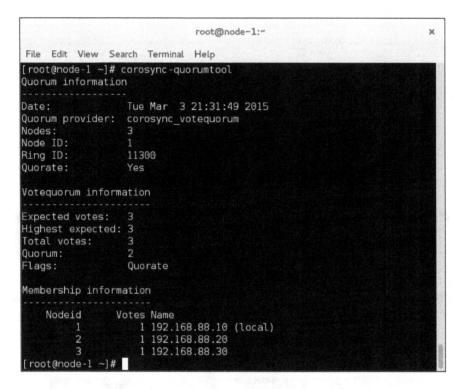

Let's take a look at the different sections of the output in more detail:

- **Quorum provider**: This parameter is the provider used for cluster Quorum
- **Nodes**: This line is where the number of your cluster nodes is listed
- **Expected votes**: This line shows the number of the expected votes in the currently active configuration

- **Highest expected**: This line shows the number of the highest expected votes possible in the currently active configuration
- **Total votes**: This line shows the number of total votes provided by the Corosync configuration file
- **Quorum**: This line shows the number of votes required to reach Quorum

Take a backup of the working Corosync configuration file, since you will need it later on. In the following screenshot, you can see the cp command used to take a backup of the Corosync configuration file:

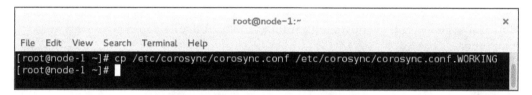

Installing and configuring Pacemaker

The party is not over yet. To finish, you need to install the pacemaker cluster manager. Before you can start the installation, you must add a firewall rule to allow Pacemaker traffic on TCP port 2224, and reload the firewall daemon. In this screenshot, you can see the commands used to add a firewall rule to allow Pacemaker traffic and reload the firewall daemon:

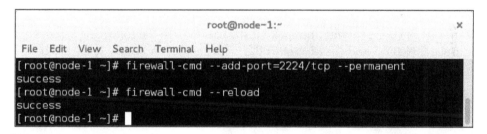

 Note that you must add a firewall rule and reload the firewall daemon on all cluster nodes.

Continue by installing Pacemaker and the `pcs` command shell. In the following screenshot, you can see the command used to install the `pacemaker` software on your system:

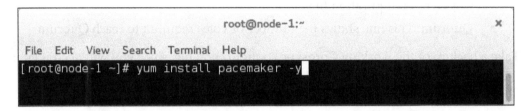

Here is a screenshot that shows the command used to make `pacemaker` start at boot time:

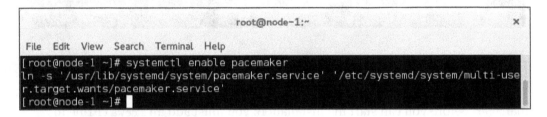

 You must install the `pacemaker` software and the `pcs` shell on all cluster nodes. Also do not forget to make Pacemaker start at boot.

You can start the `pcsd` service and make it start at boot. In the following screenshot, you can see the commands used to start the `pcsd` service and make it start at boot time:

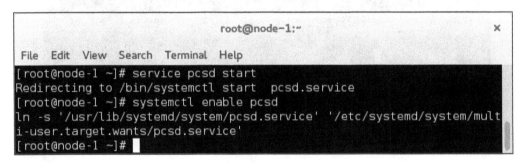

 You must start the `pcsd` service on all cluster nodes. Also do not forget to make it start at boot.

Set a password for the `hacluster` user. In this screenshot, you can see the command used to set a password for the `hacluster` user:

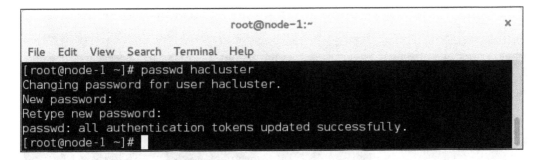

 The password for the `hacluster` user must be set on all cluster nodes. It is best if the `hacluster` user passwords are consistent (the same) across all cluster nodes; in other words, this is convenient.

The `hacluster` user is used to authenticate the `pcs` daemon across the cluster nodes. You must issue a `pcs cluster auth` command to authenticate the cluster node's `pcs` daemons. In the following screenshot, you can see the command used to authenticate the cluster node's `pcs` daemons:

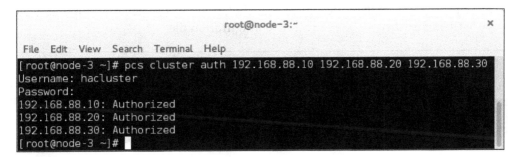

 Use the IP address when listing the cluster nodes. One of the last steps to perform is setting up your cluster.

In this screenshot, you can see the command used to set up the cluster for the first time:

```
                              root@node-1:~                          ×

 File  Edit  View  Search  Terminal  Help
[root@node-1 ~]# pcs cluster setup --name hacluster 192.168.88.10 192.168.88.20
192.168.88.30 --force
Shutting down pacemaker/corosync services...
Redirecting to /bin/systemctl stop  pacemaker.service
Redirecting to /bin/systemctl stop  corosync.service
Killing any remaining services...
Removing all cluster configuration files...
192.168.88.10: Succeeded
192.168.88.20: Succeeded
192.168.88.30: Succeeded
[root@node-1 ~]#
```

The cluster setup will generate a new Corosync configuration file and distribute it across all nodes.

The --force parameter must be used because the Corosync configuration file already exists.

Overwrite the new Corosync configuration file with the one you backed up in the previous paragraph. In the following screenshot, you can see the cp command used to overwrite an existing corosync.conf configuration file:

```
                              root@node-1:~                          ×

 File  Edit  View  Search  Terminal  Help
[root@node-1 ~]# cp /root/corosync.conf.WORKING /etc/corosync/corosync.conf
cp: overwrite '/etc/corosync/corosync.conf'? y
[root@node-1 ~]#
```

Distribute the Corosync configuration file across the other cluster nodes. In this screenshot, you can see the corosync.conf file transferred with the scp command from **node-1** to **node-2** and **node-3**:

```
                              root@node-1:~                          ×

 File  Edit  View  Search  Terminal  Help
[root@node-1 ~]# scp /etc/corosync/corosync.conf node-2:/etc/corosync/corosync.conf
corosync.conf                                 100%  762    0.7KB/s   00:00
[root@node-1 ~]# scp /etc/corosync/corosync.conf node-3:/etc/corosync/corosync.conf
corosync.conf                                 100%  762    0.7KB/s   00:00
[root@node-1 ~]#
```

Once you have transferred the Corosync configuration file to the other cluster nodes, you must change the `bindnetaddr` parameter on the cluster nodes to match the IP address of the cluster node.

Start the cluster on all the cluster nodes with a single command. In the following screenshot, you can see the command used to start the cluster on all cluster nodes:

```
                              root@node-1:~                              ×

 File   Edit   View   Search   Terminal   Help
[root@node-1 ~]# pcs cluster start --all
192.168.88.20: Starting Cluster...
192.168.88.30: Starting Cluster...
192.168.88.10: Starting Cluster...
[root@node-1 ~]# s
```

Continue by checking the cluster status with the `pcs status` command. In this screenshot, you can see the command used to check the cluster status:

```
                              root@node-1:~                              ×

 File   Edit   View   Search   Terminal   Help
[root@node-1 ~]# pcs status
Cluster name:
WARNING: no stonith devices and stonith-enabled is not false
Last updated: Tue Mar  3 22:49:21 2015
Last change: Tue Mar  3 22:47:28 2015 via crmd on node-3.geekpeek.net
Stack: corosync
Current DC: node-1.geekpeek.net (1) - partition with quorum
Version: 1.1.10-32.el7_0.1-368c726
3 Nodes configured
0 Resources configured


Online: [ node-1.geekpeek.net node-2.geekpeek.net node-3.geekpeek.net ]

Full list of resources:


PCSD Status:
   192.168.88.10: Online
   192.168.88.20: Online
   192.168.88.30: Online

Daemon Status:
   corosync: active/enabled
   pacemaker: active/enabled
   pcsd: active/enabled
[root@node-1 ~]#
```

Let's take a look at the following terms that appear in the output:

- **WARNING**: This line tells you that there are no STONITH devices configured. We will get to that later on; just ignore it for now.

- **Current DC**: This line tells us which cluster node is currently the domain controller.

- **Nodes Configured**: This parameter shows the number of nodes configured in the cluster.

- **Resources configured**: This is the number of resources configured in the cluster.

- **Online**: This line gives information about online and active cluster node members.

- **PCSD Status**: This is the `pcsd` daemon status on all configured cluster nodes.

- **Daemon Status**: This is the current state of the services. If any of these services is in the `disabled` state, make sure you make it start at boot.

All the cluster nodes must be listed and online, confirming that the cluster stack software installation and configuration on CentOS 7 were successful.

Summary

In this chapter, we covered operating system preparation and cluster stack software installation on CentOS 7. We also provided a step-by-step guide on how to install and configure the Corosync cluster messaging software and the Pacemaker cluster resource management software with the `pcs` shell. We ended the chapter with the operational configuration of the Pacemaker cluster, ready to configure and provide the cluster service. In the next chapter, we will proceed with configuring cluster resources and cluster resource groups, and managing them around the cluster.

10
Resource Manager on CentOS 7

This chapter covers cluster resource management on CentOS 7 with the Pacemaker cluster resource manager software. The Pacemaker cluster resource manager comes with a command-line tool called pcs. You will now learn how to find the information you require about the cluster resources supported by Pacemaker and all the details about cluster resource configuration. You will also learn how to add, delete, and reconfigure resources and services in your cluster. Then you will be familiarized with how to start, stop, and migrate resources from one host to another. When we are finished with this chapter, our cluster will be configured to run and provide a service for end users.

Working with pcs

pcs is short for **Pacemaker Configuration System**. It is a command-line tool that allows you to view and modify a cluster configuration. The pcs command enables you to make changes to the Corosync and Pacemaker configurations, and therefore control the cluster resources, services, and nodes. The pcs command-line syntax is as follows:

```
pcs <parameters>
```

The parameters used with the pcs command can have many levels, meaning that the following syntax can apply:

```
pcs <parameter1> <parameter2>
```

The pcs command-line help is well documented and very useful. We can get help about the pcs command usage on every level in depth, as follows:

```
pcs <parameter1> <parameter2> --help
```

The pcs command is normally used to control and reconfigure the currently active cluster configuration, but it can can also be used to perform actions on a specific cluster configuration file with the -f path_to_file option:

```
pcs -f path_to_file <parameters>
```

The pcs command-line tool allows you to perform the following actions:

- **Configure cluster options and nodes (parameter: cluster)**: The cluster parameter allows us to authenticate the nodes we want to use in our cluster. It also allows us to configure cluster timeout, redundant ring protocols, and Quorum options.

- **Manage cluster resources (parameter: resource)**: The resource parameter allows us to add new cluster resources to our cluster. It also allows us to manage cluster resources by enabling, disabling, or moving them around the cluster.

- **Configure fence devices (parameter: stonith)**: The stonith parameter enables us to configure fencing devices to be used in our cluster and manage cluster nodes with fence devices.

- **Set resource constraints (parameter: constraint)**: The constraint parameter enables us to group cluster resources; we can also configure the cluster resource, start and stop order, and preferred resource location.

- **Set pacemaker properties (parameter: property)**: The property parameter allows us to configure the cluster behavior in specific situations that may occur, such as the loss of Quorum, missing STONITH resources, and so on.

- **View cluster status (parameter: status)**: The status parameter shows the current cluster and resource status.

- **Print full cluster configuration (parameter: config)**: The config parameter prints the complete cluster configuration in human-readable form.

If you want to validate your cluster configuration, the command-line tool to use is crm_verify. The crm_verify tool allows us to check the current cluster configuration for errors.

The crm_verify syntax is as follows:

```
crm_verify -L -V
```

The -L parameter tells the crm_verify command to check the live, or currently running, cluster configuration.

The -V parameter tells the crm_verify command to increase the debug output.

We can also use the `crm_verify` command to check a specific cluster configuration file with the `-x path_to_file` option, as follows:

```
crm_verify -x path_to_xml_file -V
```

Adding cluster resources, constraints, and resource groups

In the previous chapter, we successfully installed and configured Corosync and Pacemaker on CentOS 7 and got our cluster running. Before you start adding resources, you must disable the STONITH option by issuing the following command:

```
pcs property set stonith-enabled=false
```

> STONITH is a cluster node fencing feature and is enabled by default. There is a whole chapter that is dedicated to the STONITH fencing configuration, so we will currently disable the STONITH option and get back to it later on.
>
> Note that the STONITH option should always be enabled in production systems.

Validate your cluster configuration. The output of the `crm_verify` command should be without any errors. In the following screenshot, we can see the `crm_verify` command used to check the cluster configuration for errors:

```
                              root@node-1:~                               ×

 File   Edit   View   Search   Terminal   Help
[root@node-1 ~]# crm_verify -L -V
[root@node-1 ~]# 
```

Configuring resources

Currently, your cluster is lacking resources. It is time to learn how to add new resources to your cluster.

The syntax used to add a new cluster resource is as follows:

```
pcs resource create <resource_name> <resource_type> <resource_options>
```

The `resource_name` parameter is a unique cluster resource name.

The `resource_type` parameter is the full name of the resource with resource class and resource ID.

The `resource_options` parameter contains available options to be used with the resource.

The following command provides more information on resource creation:

```
pcs resource create --help
```

There are six resource classes supported by Pacemaker, as follows:

- **OCF (Open Cluster Framework)**: This is an extension of the LSB conventions for `init` scripts and is the most preferred resource class for use in the cluster

- **LSB (Linux Standard Base)**:These are the standard Linux `init` scripts found in the `/etc/init.d` directory

- **Upstart**: This is the resource class for distributions that use upstart

- **Systemd**: This is the resource class for distributions that use the `systemd` command

- **Fencing**: This is the resource class used exclusively for fencing-related resources

- **Service**: This is the resource class to be used in the mixed cluster environments where cluster nodes use the `systemd`, `upstart`, and `lsb` commands

- **Nagios**: This is the resource class used exclusively for `Nagios` plugins

The OCF resource class is designed with strict definitions of the exit codes that actions must return, and is therefore the best and the most commonly used resource class in cluster environments.

We can get a full list of supported OCF resource classes with the following command:

```
pcs resource list heartbeat
```

We can download the output of the `pcs resource list heartbeat` command from the `command-1.txt` file from the code bundle.

Suppose we want to configure an IPv4 cluster's IP address. We can see from the OCF resource list that there are two IP address OCF resource agents we can choose from, as follows:

- `ocf:heartbeat:Ipaddr`: This manages virtual IPv4 and IPv6 addresses (Linux-specific version)

- `ocf:heartbeat:IPaddr2`: This manages virtual IPv4 and IPv6 addresses (Linux-specific version)

> The difference between the two is that the `Ipaddr` parameter uses the `ifconfig` command to create the interface and the `IPaddr2` parameter uses the `ip` command to create the interface.
>
> When running on CentOS 7, the preferable resource is the `IPaddr2` parameter.

All the resource options are well documented and explained. Reading the resource documentation will give you an idea about the resource options you might prefer to use. We can get more detailed information about the `ocf:heartbeat:IPaddr2` resource and options with the following command:

```
pcs resource describe ocf:heartbeat:IPaddr2
```

We can add an IPv4 cluster IP resource and make it bind to the network interface `enp0s8` with the following command:

```
pcs resource create ClusterIP ocf:heartbeat:IPaddr2 ip=192.168.88.50
cidr_netmask=24 nic=enp0s8
```

> - `pcs resource create`: This tells the cluster we are creating a new cluster resource
> - `ClusterIP`: This is a unique cluster resource name
> - `ofc:heartbeat:IPaddr2`: This is the OFC cluster resource agent
> - `ip=192.168.88.50`: This is the cluster IP addresses
> - `cidr_netmask=24`: This is the IP address network mask
> - `nic=enp0s8`: This is the network interface you want to bind the IP address to

The result of the command should be a new started cluster IP resource as follows. In the following screenshot you can see the output of the command `pcs status`.

```
                              root@node-1:~                               x

 File  Edit  View  Search  Terminal  Help
[root@node-1 ~]# pcs resource create ClusterIP ocf:heartbeat:IPaddr2 ip=192.168.
88.50 cidr_netmask=24 nic=enp0s8
[root@node-1 ~]# pcs status
Cluster name:
Last updated: Fri Jan 23 21:25:56 2015
Last change: Fri Jan 23 21:25:53 2015 via cibadmin on node-1.geekpeek.net
Stack: corosync
Current DC: node-1.geekpeek.net (3232258058) - partition with quorum
Version: 1.1.10-32.el7_0.1-368c726
3 Nodes configured
1 Resources configured


Online: [ node-1.geekpeek.net node-2.geekpeek.net node-3.geekpeek.net ]

Full list of resources:

 ClusterIP      (ocf::heartbeat:IPaddr2):       Started node-1.geekpeek.net

PCSD Status:
    192.168.88.10: Online
    192.168.88.20: Online
    192.168.88.30: Online

Daemon Status:
    corosync: active/enabled
    pacemaker: active/enabled
    pcsd: active/enabled
[root@node-1 ~]#
```

 As you can see in the previous screenshot, under the **Full list of resources** section, the cluster resource called **Cluster IP** with the **ocf:heartbeat:IPaddr2** resource agent was added to the cluster and started on the **node-1.geekpeek.net** cluster node.

We can continue by adding an Apache web server cluster resource. Looking at the OCF resource agent list you can find the following Apache OCF resource agent:

- `ocf:heartbeat:apache`: This Manages an Apache Web server instance

 For additional information about the Apache resource and options, run the `pcs resource describe apache` command.

We can add an Apache web server cluster resource with the following command:

```
pcs resource create WebServer ocf:heartbeat:apache configfile=/etc/httpd/
conf/httpd.conf
```

- `pcs resource create`: This tells the cluster we are creating a new cluster resource
- `WebServer`: This is a unique cluster resource name
- `ocf:heartbeat:apache`: This is the OCF cluster resource agent
- `configfile=/etc/httpd/conf/httpd.conf`: This is the Apache configuration file to use

The result of the previous command should be a new Apache web server cluster resource as follows. In the following screenshot, we can see the output of the `pcs status` command.

```
                              root@node-1:~                              x

  File  Edit  View  Search  Terminal  Help
[root@node-1 ~]# pcs resource create WebServer ocf:heartbeat:apache configfile=/etc/httpd/c
onf/httpd.conf
[root@node-1 ~]# pcs status
Cluster name:
Last updated: Fri Jan 23 21:55:31 2015
Last change: Fri Jan 23 21:49:37 2015 via cibadmin on node-1.geekpeek.net
Stack: corosync
Current DC: node-1.geekpeek.net (3232258058) - partition with quorum
Version: 1.1.10-32.el7_0.1-368c726
3 Nodes configured
2 Resources configured


Online: [ node-1.geekpeek.net node-2.geekpeek.net node-3.geekpeek.net ]

Full list of resources:

  ClusterIP     (ocf::heartbeat:IPaddr2):     Started node-1.geekpeek.net
  WebServer     (ocf::heartbeat:apache):      Started node-2.geekpeek.net

PCSD Status:
  192.168.88.10: Online
  192.168.88.20: Online
  192.168.88.30: Online

Daemon Status:
  corosync: active/enabled
  pacemaker: active/enabled
  pcsd: active/enabled
[root@node-1 ~]#
```

As you can see in the previous screenshot under the **Full list of resources** section, the cluster resource called **WebServer** with the **ocf:heartbeat:apache** resource agent was added to the cluster and started on the **node-2.geekpeek.net** cluster node.

We can now list all of the configured cluster resources with the following command:

```
pcs resource show
```

In the following screenshot, we can see the command used to list the configured cluster resources:

```
root@node-1:~                                          x

File  Edit  View  Search  Terminal  Help
[root@node-1 ~]# pcs resource show
 WebServer      (ocf::heartbeat:apache):            Started
 ClusterIP      (ocf::heartbeat:IPaddr2):           Started
[root@node-1 ~]#
```

Configuring resource constraints

Configuring cluster resource constraints is an important cluster feature since there are certain rules we want our cluster resources to apply. Cluster resource constraints cover the rules regarding the resource location, order, and colocation. Colocation is a rule binding two cluster resources to run on the same location. Usually more than one resource defines a cluster service and these resources must be running on the same cluster node. Sometimes we would also like to configure a preferred location for specific cluster resources and resource groups to run on and the start and stop order of the resources in a resource group is almost always necessary.

The following cluster resource constraints can be configured in a Pacemaker cluster:

- **Location constraint**: By configuring a resource location constraint, we prefer that the resource is running on a specific cluster node. The following command provides more information:

  ```
  pcs constraint location --help
  ```

- **Order constraint**: By configuring a resource order constraint, we configure the start and stop order for the resources. The following command provides more information:

  ```
  pcs constraint order --help
  ```

- **Colocation constraint**: By configuring colocation constraint a cluster resource group will always be running on the same cluster node. The following command provides more information:

  ```
  pcs constraint colocation --help
  ```

We can see from one of the previous screenshots that the **ClusterIP** and **WebServer** cluster resources are started on different cluster nodes. The divided resources cannot provide a desired cluster service and the only way to fix this is to configure a cluster resource colocation constraint.

We can configure **ClusterIP** and **WebServer** resource colocation constraint with the following command:

```
pcs constraint colocation add ClusterIP WebServer
```

The result of the previous command is that both cluster resources **ClusterIP** and **WebServer** are now running on the same cluster node as follows. In the following screenshot, we can see the cluster status command output:

```
                               root@node-1:~                                    ×

  File  Edit  View  Search  Terminal  Help
[root@node-1 ~]# pcs constraint colocation add ClusterIP WebServer
[root@node-1 ~]# pcs status
Cluster name:
Last updated: Fri Jan 23 23:17:49 2015
Last change: Fri Jan 23 23:17:40 2015 via cibadmin on node-1.geekpeek.net
Stack: corosync
Current DC: node-1.geekpeek.net (3232258058) - partition with quorum
Version: 1.1.10-32.el7_0.1-368c726
3 Nodes configured
2 Resources configured


Online: [ node-1.geekpeek.net node-2.geekpeek.net node-3.geekpeek.net ]

Full list of resources:

 ClusterIP      (ocf::heartbeat:IPaddr2):       Started node-1.geekpeek.net
 WebServer      (ocf::heartbeat:apache):        Started node-1.geekpeek.net

PCSD Status:
   192.168.88.10: Online
   192.168.88.20: Online
   192.168.88.30: Online

Daemon Status:
   corosync: active/enabled
   pacemaker: active/enabled
   pcsd: active/enabled
[root@node-1 ~]# ▊
```

 As you can see in the previous screenshot under the **Full list of resources** section, the cluster resources **ClusterIP** and **WebServer** have now started on the same **node-1.geekpeek.net** cluster node.

We can see the configured cluster resource colocation constraints with the following command:

```
pcs constraint colocation show
```

In the following screenshot we can see the output of the pcs constraint colocation show command:

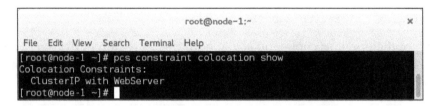

To provide a working Apache web server cluster service, the **ClusterIP** resource must be started before the **WebServer** resource. We can achieve this by configuring a cluster resource order constraint with the following command:

```
pcs constraint order set ClusterIP WebServer
```

We can see the configured cluster resource order constraints with the following command:

```
pcs constraint order show
```

In the following screenshot, we can see the output of the pcs constraint order show" command:

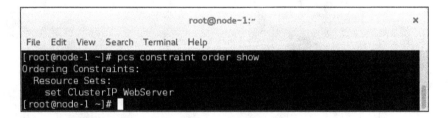

Configuring resource groups

Configuring cluster resource groups is very useful since this enables you to manage a group of resources simply by managing the resource group rather than every individual cluster resource. The following command provides more information about configuring cluster resource groups:

```
pcs resource group --help
```

You can configure a resource group called **WebSite** consisting of **ClusterIP** and **WebServer** cluster resources with the following command:

```
pcs resource group add WebSite ClusterIP WebServer
```

In the following screenshot, you can see the output of cluster status command:

```
                              root@node-1:~                              ×

 File  Edit  View  Search  Terminal  Help
[root@node-1 ~]# pcs resource group add WebSite ClusterIP WebServer
[root@node-1 ~]# pcs status
Cluster name:
Last updated: Fri Jan 23 23:39:56 2015
Last change: Fri Jan 23 23:39:48 2015 via cibadmin on node-1.geekpeek.net
Stack: corosync
Current DC: node-1.geekpeek.net (3232258058) - partition with quorum
Version: 1.1.10-32.el7_0.1-368c726
3 Nodes configured
2 Resources configured


Online: [ node-1.geekpeek.net node-2.geekpeek.net node-3.geekpeek.net ]

Full list of resources:

 Resource Group: WebSite
     ClusterIP   (ocf::heartbeat:IPaddr2):      Started node-1.geekpeek.net
     WebServer   (ocf::heartbeat:apache):       Started node-1.geekpeek.net

PCSD Status:
  192.168.88.10: Online
  192.168.88.20: Online
  192.168.88.30: Online

Daemon Status:
  corosync: active/enabled
  pacemaker: active/enabled
  pcsd: active/enabled
[root@node-1 ~]# █
```

 As you can see in the previous screenshot under the **Full list of resources** section, the resource group called **WebSite** is configured and consists of two cluster resources **ClusterIP** and **WebServer**.

Once you have configured a cluster resource group, you can proceed to manage the cluster resource group instead of managing individual cluster resources.

Managing resources

You can manage the configured cluster resources in many ways. The following actions can apply:

- **Start resource (syntax: pcs resource enable <resource_name> --wait=[n])**: Start a non running cluster resource where the --wait parameter is optional and n is the number of seconds to wait for the resource to start. The following command provides more information:

  ```
  pcs resource enable --help
  ```

- **Stop resource (syntax: pcs resource disable <resource_name> --wait=[n])**: Start a running cluster resource where the --wait parameter is optional and n is the number of seconds to wait for the resource to stop. The following command provides more information:

  ```
  pcs resource disable --help
  ```

- **Debug start resource (syntax: pcs resource debug-start <resource_name> --full)**: Start a non running cluster resource on the current node; ignoring the cluster recommendations where the --full parameter is optional will give a more detailed output. The following command provides more information:

  ```
  pcs resource debug-start --help
  ```

- **Move resource (syntax: pcs resource move <resource_name> <cluster_node>)**: Move the cluster resource to the specified cluster node. The following command provides more information:

  ```
  pcs resource move --help
  ```

 Please note that moving the cluster resource around the cluster automatically creates resource location constraints.

- **Ban resource (syntax: pcs resource ban <resource_name> <cluster_node>)**: Ban the cluster resource and prevent it from running on the specified cluster node. If no cluster node is specified, you ban the resource from running on the current cluster node. The following command provides more information:

  ```
  pcs resource ban -help7
  ```

- **Clear resource (syntax: pcs resource clear <resource_name>)**: Remove constraints created by the move or ban resource command. The following command provides more information:

  ```
  pcs resource clear --help
  ```

Moving resources around

You can move the cluster resource group called **WebSite** from the example running on **node-1.geekpeek.net** to **node-2.geekpeek.net** with the following command:

```
pcs resource move WebSite node-3.geekpeek.net
```

In the following screenshot, you can see the output of the cluster status command after successfully moving the **WebSite** cluster resource to the **node-3.geekpeek.net** cluster node.

```
                             root@node-1:~                              ×

 File  Edit  View  Search  Terminal  Help
[root@node-1 ~]# pcs resource move WebSite node-3.geekpeek.net
[root@node-1 ~]# pcs status
Cluster name:
Last updated: Sat Jan 24 21:37:25 2015
Last change: Sat Jan 24 21:36:32 2015 via crm_resource on node-1.geekpeek.net
Stack: corosync
Current DC: node-2.geekpeek.net (3232258068) - partition with quorum
Version: 1.1.10-32.el7_0.1-368c726
3 Nodes configured
2 Resources configured


Online: [ node-1.geekpeek.net node-2.geekpeek.net node-3.geekpeek.net ]

Full list of resources:

 Resource Group: WebSite
     ClusterIP   (ocf::heartbeat:IPaddr2):       Started node-3.geekpeek.net
     WebServer   (ocf::heartbeat:apache):        Started node-3.geekpeek.net

PCSD Status:
   192.168.88.10: Online
   192.168.88.20: Online
   192.168.88.30: Online

Daemon Status:
   corosync: active/enabled
   pacemaker: active/enabled
   pcsd: active/enabled
[root@node-1 ~]#
```

 As you can see in the previous screenshot under the **Full list of resources** section, the resource group called **WebSite** was moved from **node-1.geekpeek.net** to **node-3.geekpeek.net**.

Stopping resources

You usually want to stop the cluster resource when you want to reconfigure it or do some maintenance work on it. You can stop the **WebSite** cluster resource with the following command:

```
pcs resource disable WebSite
```

In the following screenshot, you can see the output of the cluster status command after successfully stopping the **WebSite** cluster resource:

```
                              root@node-1:~                                    ×

 File  Edit  View  Search  Terminal  Help
[root@node-1 ~]# pcs resource disable WebSite
[root@node-1 ~]# pcs status
Cluster name:
Last updated: Sat Jan 24 21:42:33 2015
Last change: Sat Jan 24 21:42:08 2015 via crm_resource on node-1.geekpeek.net
Stack: corosync
Current DC: node-2.geekpeek.net (3232258068) - partition with quorum
Version: 1.1.10-32.el7_0.1-368c726
3 Nodes configured
2 Resources configured


Online: [ node-1.geekpeek.net node-2.geekpeek.net node-3.geekpeek.net ]

Full list of resources:

 Resource Group: WebSite
     ClusterIP  (ocf::heartbeat:IPaddr2):        Stopped
     WebServer  (ocf::heartbeat:apache):         Stopped

PCSD Status:
   192.168.88.10: Online
   192.168.88.20: Online
   192.168.88.30: Online

Daemon Status:
   corosync: active/enabled
   pacemaker: active/enabled
   pcsd: active/enabled
[root@node-1 ~]#
```

 As you can see in the preceding screenshot under the **Full list of resources** section, the resource group called **WebSite** was successfully stopped.

Starting resources

When the cluster resource maintenance work is done, you can start the cluster resource **WebSite** again with the following command:

```
pcs resource enable WebSite
```

In the following screenshot, you can see the output of the cluster status command after successfully starting the **WebSite** cluster resource.

```
                              root@node-1:~                                      x

 File  Edit  View  Search  Terminal  Help
[root@node-1 ~]# pcs resource enable WebSite
[root@node-1 ~]# pcs status
Cluster name:
Last updated: Sat Jan 24 21:44:42 2015
Last change: Sat Jan 24 21:44:33 2015 via crm_resource on node-1.geekpeek.net
Stack: corosync
Current DC: node-2.geekpeek.net (3232258068) - partition with quorum
Version: 1.1.10-32.el7_0.1-368c726
3 Nodes configured
2 Resources configured


Online: [ node-1.geekpeek.net node-2.geekpeek.net node-3.geekpeek.net ]

Full list of resources:

 Resource Group: WebSite
     ClusterIP  (ocf::heartbeat:IPaddr2):        Started node-3.geekpeek.net
     WebServer  (ocf::heartbeat:apache):         Started node-3.geekpeek.net

PCSD Status:
   192.168.88.10: Online
   192.168.88.20: Online
   192.168.88.30: Online

Daemon Status:
   corosync: active/enabled
   pacemaker: active/enabled
   pcsd: active/enabled
[root@node-1 ~]#
```

> As you can see in the preceding screenshot under the **Full list of resources** section, the resource group called **WebSite** was successfully started on the **node-3.geekpeek.net** cluster node.

Banning resources

Banning a cluster resource is useful when you want to prevent it from running on a specific cluster node. You can ban the **WebSite** cluster resource from running on the **node-1.geekpeek.net** cluster node with the following command:

```
pcs resource ban WebSite node-1.geekpeek.net
```

Clearing resource constraints

When moving cluster resources around the cluster, the location constraints are automatically appended to the resources. This is when clearing cluster resource constraint, comes in handy. You can clear the cluster resource **WebSite** location constraint automatically configured when moving it to the **node-1.geekpeek.net** cluster node, with the following command:

```
pcs resource clear WebSite node-1.geekpeek.net
```

Removing cluster constraints, resource groups, and resources

Knowing how to remove the configured cluster constraints, resource groups, and resources is just as important as knowing how to configure them. Removing them is quite easy and self-explanatory.

Removing resource constraints

You can see the configured cluster resource constraints with the following command:

```
pcs constraint show
```

In the following screenshot, you can see the output of the `pcs constraint show` command.

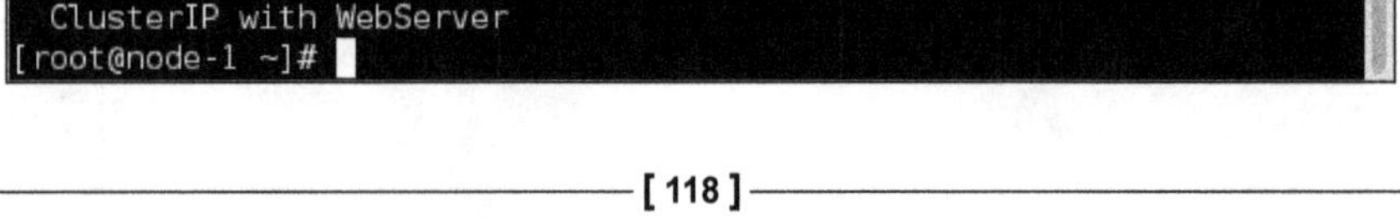

```
root@node-1:~                                    ×

File  Edit  View  Search  Terminal  Help
[root@node-1 ~]# pcs constraint show
Location Constraints:
Ordering Constraints:
  Resource Sets:
    set ClusterIP WebServer
Colocation Constraints:
  ClusterIP with WebServer
[root@node-1 ~]#
```

As you can see in the preceding screenshot, the possible configured location constraints are:

- **Location constraints**: None configured
- **Ordering constraints**: The cluster resource order constraint is set to start the resource called **ClusterIP** before the resource called **WebServer**
- **Colocation constraints**: The cluster resource colocation constraint is configured to run resources **ClusterIP** and **WebServer** together
- You can delete the cluster order constraint from the preceding example with the following command:

  ```
  pcs constraint order remove ClusterIP WebServer
  ```

- If you would like to delete the cluster colocation constraint from the example, you can do that with the following command:

  ```
  pcs constraint colocation remove WebServer ClusterIP
  ```

- In the following screenshot, you can see the output of the `pcs constraint show` command after deleting all of the configured constraints.

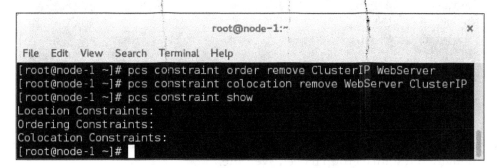

Removing resource groups

You can see the configured cluster resource groups with the following command:

```
pcs status
```

In the following screenshot, you can see the output of the cluster status command:

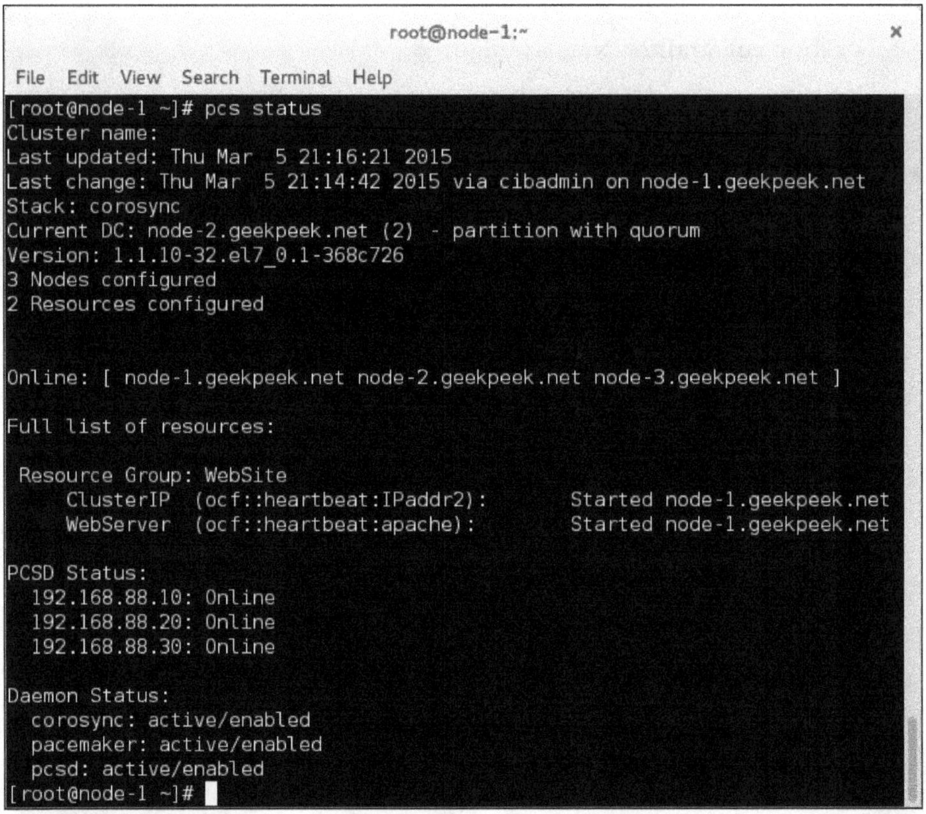

```
                              root@node-1:~                                    ×

 File  Edit  View  Search  Terminal  Help
[root@node-1 ~]# pcs status
Cluster name:
Last updated: Thu Mar  5 21:16:21 2015
Last change: Thu Mar  5 21:14:42 2015 via cibadmin on node-1.geekpeek.net
Stack: corosync
Current DC: node-2.geekpeek.net (2) - partition with quorum
Version: 1.1.10-32.el7_0.1-368c726
3 Nodes configured
2 Resources configured


Online: [ node-1.geekpeek.net node-2.geekpeek.net node-3.geekpeek.net ]

Full list of resources:

 Resource Group: WebSite
     ClusterIP  (ocf::heartbeat:IPaddr2):        Started node-1.geekpeek.net
     WebServer  (ocf::heartbeat:apache):         Started node-1.geekpeek.net

PCSD Status:
   192.168.88.10: Online
   192.168.88.20: Online
   192.168.88.30: Online

Daemon Status:
   corosync: active/enabled
   pacemaker: active/enabled
   pcsd: active/enabled
[root@node-1 ~]#
```

As you can see in the preceding screenshot in the **Full list of resources** section, there is a configured resource group named **WebSite**.

You can remove the resource group from the cluster example with the following command:

```
pcs resource group remove WebSite
```

In the following image you can see the cluster status command after successfully removing a **WebSite** resource group.

```
                          root@node-1:~                            ×

  File  Edit  View  Search  Terminal  Help
[root@node-1 ~]# pcs resource group remove WebSite
[root@node-1 ~]# pcs status
Cluster name:
Last updated: Thu Mar  5 21:20:27 2015
Last change: Thu Mar  5 21:20:18 2015 via cibadmin on node-1.geekpeek.net
Stack: corosync
Current DC: node-2.geekpeek.net (2) - partition with quorum
Version: 1.1.10-32.el7_0.1-368c726
3 Nodes configured
2 Resources configured


Online: [ node-1.geekpeek.net node-2.geekpeek.net node-3.geekpeek.net ]

Full list of resources:

 ClusterIP       (ocf::heartbeat:IPaddr2):       Started node-1.geekpeek.net
 WebServer       (ocf::heartbeat:apache):        Started node-2.geekpeek.net

PCSD Status:
   192.168.88.10: Online
   192.168.88.20: Online
   192.168.88.30: Online

Daemon Status:
   corosync: active/enabled
   pacemaker: active/enabled
   pcsd: active/enabled
[root@node-1 ~]#
```

 As you can see in the preceding screenshot the resource group called **WebSite** was successfully removed from the cluster configuration.

Removing resources

You see the configured cluster resources by running the following command:

`pcs resource show`

In the following screenshot, you can see the output of the `pcs resource show` command.

 As you can see in the preceding screenshot, there are two cluster resources configured in the cluster, called **ClusterIP** and **WebServer**.

You can remove the cluster resource called **ClusterIP** with the following command:

```
pcs resource delete ClusterIP
```

You can remove the cluster resource called **WebServer** with the following command:

```
pcs resource delete WebServer
```

In the following screenshot, you can see the output of the `pcs resource show` command after successfully removing the **ClusterIP** and **WebServer** cluster resources.

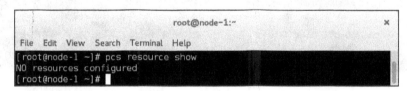

 As you can see in the preceding screenshot, both cluster resources **ClusterIP** and **WebServer** were removed from the cluster configuration.

Summary

In this chapter, you learned how to configure cluster resources and resource groups with the Pacemaker configuration system. You also learned how to configure cluster resource location, colocation, and order constraints. To finish up, you learned how to list and remove configured resources, resource groups, and resource constraints. In the following chapter you will start playing around with cluster nodes, adding and removing them from the active cluster configuration.

11
Playing with Cluster Nodes on CentOS 7

In the previous chapter, you learned to configure and manage cluster resources and services. Now it is time you learned how to manage cluster nodes. In this chapter, you will learn how to add a new cluster node to the cluster, put a cluster node on standby, and remove a cluster node from your cluster on CentOS 7. When you are done with this chapter, managing cluster nodes on CentOS 7 will be a breeze for you.

Adding a new cluster node

Adding a new cluster node to the existing cluster configuration does not require any cluster service downtime. You should be familiar with the process of installing and configuring cluster stack software on a CentOS 7 cluster node from *Chapter 9, Cluster Stack Software on CentOS 7*. Therefore, the steps for adding a new cluster node are not covered in detail.

Follow these steps to add a new cluster node to the running cluster configuration:

1. **Operating system preparation**:
   - Configure the network interfaces and networking
   - Configure the NTP time synchronization
   - Configure the DNS resolving
   - Check network connectivity between the cluster nodes

 For a details on how to prepare the operating system for CentOS 7, refer to *Chapter 9, Cluster Stack Software on CentOS 7*.

2. **Install and configure Corosync:**

- ○ Install Corosync on the new cluster node and configure the firewall to allow Corosync cluster communication.

- ○ Transfer the `corosync.conf` configuration file and the `authkey` authentication key from a preexisting cluster node to the new cluster node. In the following screenshot, you can see the `scp` command used to transfer the `corosync.conf` configuration file and `authkey` to the **node-4.geekpeek.net** cluster node:

```
                         root@node-1:~                              ×

 File  Edit  View  Search  Terminal  Help
[root@node-1 ~]# scp /etc/corosync/corosync.conf node-4:/etc/corosync/
corosync.conf                        100%  421        0.4KB/s   00:00
[root@node-1 ~]# scp /etc/corosync/authkey node-4:/etc/corosync/
authkey                              100%  128        0.1KB/s   00:00
[root@node-1 ~]#
```

- ○ Edit the Corosync configuration file on the new cluster node and change the `bindnetaddr` parameter accordingly. The `bindnetaddr` parameter must be changed to the **node-4.geekpeek.net** cluster node's IP address.

- ○ Edit the Corosync configuration file on all the nodes and add the new cluster node to the `nodelist` section. You can download an example cluster node Corosync configuration file from the `corosync-conf-1.txt` file in the code bundle. The `bindnetaddr` parameter was changed to the **node-4.geekpeek.net** IP address, and the new node was added to the `nodelist` section.

Remember to edit the `corosync.conf` configuration file on all the cluster nodes and add a new cluster node to the `nodelist` section.

- ○ Start the Corosync cluster service on the new cluster node. In the following screenshot, you can see the command used to start the Corosync service:

```
                          root@node-4:~                          ×

 File  Edit  View  Search  Terminal  Help
[root@node-4 ~]# service corosync start
Redirecting to /bin/systemctl start  corosync.service
[root@node-4 ~]# █
```

 For details on how to install and configure Corosync on CentOS 7, refer to *Chapter 9, Cluster Stack Software on CentOS 7.*

3. **Install Pacemaker and pcs**:

   ° Install Pacemaker and pcs on the new cluster node, and start both of these services.

   ° Set the password for the hacluster user. In this screenshot, you can see the command used to configure a password for the hacluster user on the **node-4.geekpeek.net** cluster node:

   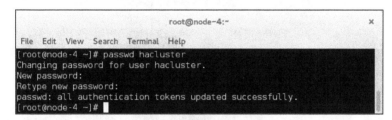

   ```
                             root@node-4:~                          ×

    File  Edit  View  Search  Terminal  Help
   [root@node-4 ~]# passwd hacluster
   Changing password for user hacluster.
   New password:
   Retype new password:
   passwd: all authentication tokens updated successfully.
   [root@node-4 ~]# █
   ```

   ° Authenticate the new cluster node's pcs daemon from all existing cluster nodes. In the following screenshot, you can see the command used to authenticate the pcs daemon from the **node-1.geekpeek.net** cluster node:

   ```
                             root@node-1:~                          ×

    File  Edit  View  Search  Terminal  Help
   [root@node-1 ~]# pcs cluster auth 192.168.88.40
   Username: hacluster
   Password:
   192.168.88.40: Authorized
   [root@node-1 ~]# █
   ```

Remember to repeat the process of pcs daemon authentication on all existing cluster nodes.

° Check the cluster status to confirm that the new cluster node has successfully joined the cluster. In this screenshot, you can see the cluster status command output with the **node-4.geekpeek.net** cluster node successfully joined to the cluster:

```
                              root@node-1:~                              x

 File  Edit  View  Search  Terminal  Help
Cluster name:
Last updated: Fri Mar  6 21:59:54 2015
Last change: Fri Mar  6 21:49:56 2015 via crm_attribute on node-1.geekpeek.net
Stack: corosync
Current DC: node-1.geekpeek.net (1) - partition with quorum
Version: 1.1.10-32.el7_0.1-368c726
4 Nodes configured
2 Resources configured


Online: [ node-1.geekpeek.net node-2.geekpeek.net node-3.geekpeek.net node-4.ge
ekpeek.net ]

Full list of resources:

 Resource Group: WebSite
     ClusterIP  (ocf::heartbeat:IPaddr2):        Started node-2.geekpeek.net
     WebServer  (ocf::heartbeat:apache):         Started node-2.geekpeek.net

PCSD Status:
  192.168.88.10: Online
  192.168.88.20: Online
  192.168.88.30: Online
  192.168.88.40: Online

Daemon Status:
  corosync: active/enabled
  pacemaker: active/enabled
  pcsd: active/enabled
[root@node-1 ~]#
```

Cluster node standby mode

Pacemaker allows you to put the desired cluster node into `standby` mode. When a cluster node is in `standby` mode, it will no longer be able to host cluster resources and services. The `standby` mode is useful for cluster node maintenance operations.

The syntax to put a cluster node in `standby` mode is as follows:

`pcs cluster standby node_name`

Here, the `node_name` parameter is the name of the cluster node you want to put in `standby` mode as it appears when running the `pcs status` command.

The following is the syntax used to take a cluster node out of `standby` mode:

`pcs cluster unstandby node_name`

Here, the `node_name` parameter is the name of the cluster node you want to take out `standby` mode as it appears when running the `pcs status` command.

You can put a cluster node called `node-4.geekpeek.net` into `standby` mode with the following command:

`pcs cluster standby node-4.geekpeek.net`

In this screenshot, you can see the command used to put the **node-4.geekpeek.net** cluster node in `standby` mode:

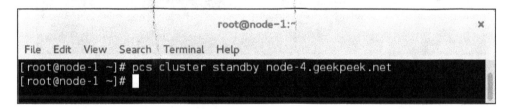

In the following screenshot, you can see the output of the cluster status command and confirm that the **node-4.geekpeek.net** cluster node is in standby mode:

```
                               root@node-1:~                              ✕

  File  Edit  View  Search  Terminal  Help
 [root@node-1 ~]# pcs status
 Cluster name:
 Last updated: Fri Mar  6 22:00:57 2015
 Last change: Fri Mar  6 22:00:52 2015 via crm_attribute on node-1.geekpeek.net
 Stack: corosync
 Current DC: node-1.geekpeek.net (1) - partition with quorum
 Version: 1.1.10-32.el7_0.1-368c726
 4 Nodes configured
 2 Resources configured


 Node node-4.geekpeek.net (4): standby
 Online: [ node-1.geekpeek.net node-2.geekpeek.net node-3.geekpeek.net ]

 Full list of resources:

  Resource Group: WebSite
     ClusterIP   (ocf::heartbeat:IPaddr2):     Started node-2.geekpeek.net
     WebServer   (ocf::heartbeat:apache):      Started node-2.geekpeek.net

 PCSD Status:
   192.168.88.10: Online
   192.168.88.20: Online
   192.168.88.30: Online
   192.168.88.40: Online

 Daemon Status:
   corosync: active/enabled
   pacemaker: active/enabled
   pcsd: active/enabled
 [root@node-1 ~]#
```

You can take a cluster node called node-4.geekpeek.net out of standby mode using the following command:

```
pcs cluster unstandby node-4.geekpeek.net
```

In this screenshot, you can see the command used to take the **node-4.geekpeek.net** cluster node out of standby mode:

```
                               root@node-1:~                              ✕

  File  Edit  View  Search  Terminal  Help
 [root@node-1 ~]# pcs cluster unstandby node-4.geekpeek.net
 [root@node-1 ~]#
```

In the following screenshot, you can see the output of the cluster status command and confirm that the **node-4.geekpeek.net** cluster node is no longer in `standby` mode:

```
                              root@node-1:~                              ×

  File  Edit  View  Search  Terminal  Help
[root@node-1 ~]# pcs status
Cluster name:
Last updated: Fri Mar  6 22:02:06 2015
Last change: Fri Mar  6 22:01:58 2015 via crm_attribute on node-1.geekpeek.net
Stack: corosync
Current DC: node-1.geekpeek.net (1) - partition with quorum
Version: 1.1.10-32.el7_0.1-368c726
4 Nodes configured
2 Resources configured


Online: [ node-1.geekpeek.net node-2.geekpeek.net node-3.geekpeek.net node-4.ge
ekpeek.net ]

Full list of resources:

  Resource Group: WebSite
      ClusterIP   (ocf::heartbeat:IPaddr2):       Started node-2.geekpeek.net
      WebServer   (ocf::heartbeat:apache):        Started node-2.geekpeek.net

PCSD Status:
    192.168.88.10: Online
    192.168.88.20: Online
    192.168.88.30: Online
    192.168.88.40: Online

Daemon Status:
  corosync: active/enabled
  pacemaker: active/enabled
  pcsd: active/enabled
[root@node-1 ~]#
```

Removing a cluster node

Shutting down a cluster node is one way to disable it, but you must also learn how to remove a cluster node from a running cluster configuration. Removing a cluster node from a cluster configuration does not require cluster service downtime, unless the cluster service is running on the cluster node you would like to remove.

 Before you start the procedure of removing a cluster node from the cluster configuration, make sure that no cluster resources and services are running on the node.

You can remove a cluster node from an existing configuration by following these steps:

1. **Remove the cluster node from Corosync**: Edit the `corosync.conf` configuration file on all cluster nodes and remove the desired cluster node from the `nodelist` section. You can download an example cluster node `corosync.conf` configuration file, where the **node-4.geekpeek.net** cluster node was removed from the cluster configuration, from the `corosync-conf-2.txt` file in the code bundle.

 Remember to remove the cluster node from the `corosync.conf` configuration file on all cluster nodes.

2. **Stop the cluster stack software**: Stop the `pcsd`, Pacemaker, and Corosync cluster services on the cluster node you want to remove from the cluster. In this screenshot, you can see the commands used to stop the `pcsd`, Pacemaker, and Corosync cluster services on the **node-4.geekpeek.net** cluster node:

```
                    root@node-4:~                    ×

 File   Edit   View   Search   Terminal   Help
[root@node-4 ~]# service pcsd stop
Redirecting to /bin/systemctl stop  pcsd.service
[root@node-4 ~]# service pacemaker stop
Redirecting to /bin/systemctl stop  pacemaker.service
[root@node-4 ~]# service corosync stop
Redirecting to /bin/systemctl stop  corosync.service
[root@node-4 ~]#
```

3. Check the cluster status. You will see that the removed cluster node **node-4.geekpeek.net** is listed as **offline**. In the following screenshot, you can see the output of the cluster status command showing the **node-4.geekpeek.net** cluster node as **offline**:

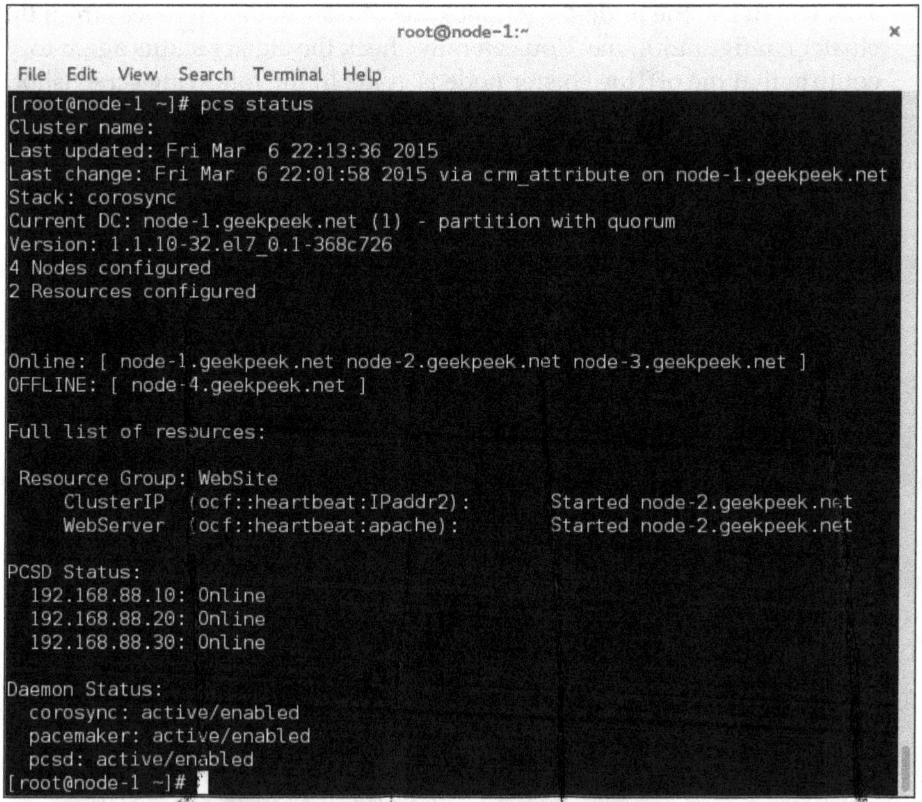

```
root@node-1:~                                              ×

File  Edit  View  Search  Terminal  Help

[root@node-1 ~]# pcs status
Cluster name:
Last updated: Fri Mar  6 22:13:36 2015
Last change: Fri Mar  6 22:01:58 2015 via crm_attribute on node-1.geekpeek.net
Stack: corosync
Current DC: node-1.geekpeek.net (1) - partition with quorum
Version: 1.1.10-32.el7_0.1-368c726
4 Nodes configured
2 Resources configured


Online: [ node-1.geekpeek.net node-2.geekpeek.net node-3.geekpeek.net ]
OFFLINE: [ node-4.geekpeek.net ]

Full list of resources:

 Resource Group: WebSite
     ClusterIP  (ocf::heartbeat:IPaddr2):        Started node-2.geekpeek.net
     WebServer  (ocf::heartbeat:apache):         Started node-2.geekpeek.net

PCSD Status:
   192.168.88.10: Online
   192.168.88.20: Online
   192.168.88.30: Online

Daemon Status:
   corosync: active/enabled
   pacemaker: active/enabled
   pcsd: active/enabled
[root@node-1 ~]#
```

4. Remove the **offline** cluster node by typing the following in the
   command line:

   ```
   cibadmin --delete --obj_type nodes --crm_xml '<node uname="node-4.
   geekpeek.net"/>'
   ```

   ```
   cibadmin --delete --obj_type status --crm_xml '<node_state
   uname="node-4.geekpeek.net"/>'
   ```

This will delete the **node-4.geekpeek.net** cluster node references from the cluster configuration file. You can now check the cluster status again to confirm that the **offline** cluster node is gone. In the following screenshot, you can see the output of the cluster status command:

```
                              root@node-1:~                              x

 File   Edit   View   Search   Terminal   Help
[root@node-1 ~]# pcs status
Cluster name:
Last updated: Fri Mar  6 22:34:16 2015
Last change: Fri Mar  6 22:31:15 2015 via cibadmin on node-1.geekpeek.net
Stack: corosync
Current DC: node-1.geekpeek.net (1) - partition with quorum
Version: 1.1.10-32.el7_0.1-368c726
3 Nodes configured
2 Resources configured


Online: [ node-1.geekpeek.net node-2.geekpeek.net node-3.geekpeek.net ]

Full list of resources:

 Resource Group: WebSite
     ClusterIP  (ocf::heartbeat:IPaddr2):        Started node-2.geekpeek.net
     WebServer  (ocf::heartbeat:apache):         Started node-2.geekpeek.net

PCSD Status:
  192.168.88.10: Online
  192.168.88.20: Online
  192.168.88.30: Online

Daemon Status:
  corosync: active/enabled
  pacemaker: active/enabled
  pcsd: active/enabled
[root@node-1 ~]#
```

Summary

In this chapter, you learned how to add a cluster node to a running cluster configuration, and how to remove a cluster node from it without any cluster service disruption or downtime. You also learned how to put a cluster in standby mode, which is particularly useful when performing maintenance work on the cluster node. In the next chapter, you will learn about the fencing mechanism and how to configure it.

12
STONITH on CentOS 7

In this chapter, you will learn how to configure and test cluster node fencing with STONITH on CentOS 7 and Pacemaker. You will become familiar with the fencing options available and learn the syntax used to configure them. You will also learn how to take your fencing configuration for a test drive and make sure it works as expected.

Fencing

Fencing is an important cluster task. It isolates a computer cluster node when the node misbehaves in order to protect the shared cluster resources and prevent cluster disruption. If you do not configure fencing, a misbehaving computer cluster node can corrupt the cluster data. This is why it is necessary to exclude the problematic cluster node from cluster configuration immediately. Corosync version 2 fencing implements some additional configurable parameters that can be applied to allow fencing configuration in a two-node cluster configuration and ensure normal operation of such a cluster. The details of this are described in *Chapter 14, Two-node Cluster Considerations on CentOS 7.*

In Pacemaker, fencing is called STONITH. **STONITH** is a fencing technique that stands for **Shoot The Other Node In The Head**. STONITH fences failed cluster nodes by rebooting or powering the node off.

The node fencing cluster feature is provided by fencing agents. Fencing agents are scripts that get executed when the cluster situation makes calls for them. Fencing agents in CentOS 7 are not installed by default when installing Pacemaker. They must be installed additionally. You can install all available fencing agents by installing the RPM package, or you can install only the fencing agents you require.

The following fencing devices are used most commonly in cluster environments:

- **APC switch**: The APC switch is a rack mount automatic transfer switch that provides power to servers. It has built-in network connectivity and enables remote management, which provides the ability to cut off the power if required.

- **Intelligent Platform Management Interface management board (IPMI)**: The IPMI interface is embedded on a server but completely independent from the server's system. It enables server monitoring and management even if the server is powered off.

- **HP iLO management board**: HP Integrated Lights-Out is also an embedded server management technology created by Hewlett Packard. It is similar to IPMI and allows administrators to remotely turn a server on and off.

- **Additional devices**: There are many additional fencing devices you can use. Additionally, the fencing agents for fencing devices can be installed as required. You can install only the fence agents you require or choose to install all available agents. Other than HP iLO, a popular server manufacturer DELL also implements a similar DRAC mechanism to support fencing.

Configuring fence devices

The first step to configuring fence devices is to check and turn on the STONITH cluster feature. You can see the status of the STONITH feature by running the `pcs property list` command. In the following screenshot, you can see the output of this command:

```
                              root@node-1:~                              ✕

   File   Edit   View   Search   Terminal   Help
  [root@node-1 ~]# pcs property list
  Cluster Properties:
   cluster-infrastructure: corosync
   dc-version: 1.1.10-32.el7_0.1-368c726
   stonith-enabled: false
  [root@node-1 ~]#
```

You can see in the **stonith-enabled** line that the STONITH feature is currently disabled.

You can enable the STONITH feature by running the `pcs property set stonith-enabled=true` command. In the following screenshot, you can see the command used to enable STONITH and the output afterwards:

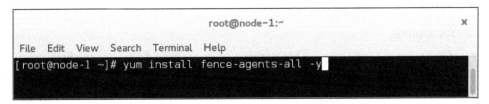

You can see in the **stonith-enabled** line that the STONITH feature is now enabled.

To continue configuring the fence devices, you must install the fence agents on all of your cluster nodes. You can install all the fencing agents available in CentOS 7 with one command. In the following screenshot, you can see the command used to install all available fencing agents:

Note that you must repeat this process on all cluster nodes.

Once you have installed the fence agents, you can get a list of all available fence agents by running the following command:

```
pcs stonith list
```

The full result of the pcs stonith list command can be downloaded from the command-1.txt file from the code bundle.

In the file from the code bundle, you can see a list of the available fence agents installed on the system by running the pcs stonith list command.

You can get detailed information about a specific fence agent by running the following command:

```
pcs stonith describe fence_agent_name
```

The result of pcs stonith describe fence_ipmilan can be downloaded from the command-2.txt file from the code bundle.

In the file from the code bundle, you can see additional information about the fencing device called `fence_ipmilan`.

Fencing devices are configured via the `pcs stonith` command. This command provides information about currently available and configured fence agents, their detailed description, and also information on fencing agent configuration and management.

You can get a detailed `pcs stonith` command usage by running this line:

```
pcs stonith -help
```

The syntax used to configure a new fence device is as follows:

```
pcs stonith create fence_name fence_agent fence_agent_options
```

Let's take a look at the following terms:

- `fence_name`: This parameter is a desired unique name of the fence device
- `fence_agent`: This parameter is the fence agent you would like to use for fencing
- `fence_agent_options`: This parameter contains additional configuration options for the chosen fence agent

APC switch fencing

If you want to configure APC switch fencing, you must know the following information:

- **APC switch IP address**: The IP address of your APC switch
- **APC switch login details**: The username and password to use to successfully connect to the APC switch
- **APC switch port connections**: From this, you can know the power port numbers specific cluster nodes are connected to

You can get information about additional APC switch fencing agent parameters by running the `pcs stonith describe fence_apc` command. You can download the output of this command from the `command-3.txt` file from the code bundle.

You can configure an APC switch fencing device with the following command:

```
pcs stonith create apcfence1 fence_apc ipaddr="192.168.88.100"
login="apcuser" passwd="apcpass" port="1" action="reboot" pcmk_host_
list="node-1.geekpeek.net"
```

Let's take a look at the following terms:

- `apcfence1`: This parameter is the unique name of a fence device
- `fence_apc`: This parameter is the fence agent to be used
- `ipaddr="192.168.88.100"`: This parameter is the IP address of the APC switch to connect to
- `login="apcuser"`: This parameter is the username used when connecting to the APC switch
- `passwd="apcpass"`: This parameter is the password used when connecting to the APC switch
- `port="1"`: This parameter is the APC switch power port to be managed
- `action="reboot"`: This parameter is the action the fencing mechanism will take
- `pcmk_host_list="node-1.geekpeek.net"`: This parameter is the cluster node managed by the corresponding fence device configuration

> Note that the fencing device that we just covered is configured to fence only the cluster node called `node-1.geekpeek.net`.

You must repeat the process of fence device configuration for all cluster nodes, as follows:

```
pcs stonith create apcfence2 fence_apc ipaddr="192.168.88.100"
login="apcuser" passwd="apcpass" port="2" action="reboot" pcmk_host_
list="node-2.geekpeek.net"
```

```
pcs stonith create apcfence3 fence_apc ipaddr="192.168.88.100"
login="apcuser" passwd="apcpass" port="3" action="reboot" pcmk_host_
list="node-3.geekpeek.net"
```

Once configured, the newly configured APC switch fencing devices should be listed as started in the **Full list of resources** that we can see on the screen after running the `pcs status` command.

```
Full list of resources:
  apcfence1   (stonith:fence_apc):   Started
  apcfence2   (stonith:fence_apc):   Started
  apcfence3   (stonith:fence_apc):   Started
```

IPMI management board fencing

To configure your cluster with IPMI management board fencing, you should know the following information:

- **IPMI IP address of each cluster node**: This is the IP address of the IPMI management board. Each cluster node has its own IPMI IP address.

- **IPMI login details for each cluster node**: These are the username and password used to successfully connect to the cluster node IPMI management board. Each cluster node can have different IPMI login details.

You can get information about additional IPMI management board fencing agent parameters by running the pcs stonith describe fence_ipmilan command. You can download the output of this command from the command-4.txt file from the code bundle.

You can configure an IPMI management board fencing device with the following command:

```
pcs stonith create ipmilan1 fence_ipmilan ipaddr="192.168.88.100"
login="ipmiuser1" passwd="ipmipass1" action="reboot" pcmk_host_
list="node-1.geekpeek.net"
```

Let's take a look at the following terms:

- ipmilan1: This parameter is the unique name of a fence device
- fence_ipmilan: This parameter is the fence agent to be used
- ipaddr="192.168.88.100": This parameter is the IP address of the IPMI management board to connect to
- login="ipmiuser1": This parameter is the username used when connecting to the IPMI management board
- passwd="ipmipass1": This parameter is the password used when connecting to the IPMI management board
- action="reboot": This parameter is the action the fencing mechanism will take
- pcmk_host_list="node-1.geekpeek.net": This parameter is the cluster node managed by the corresponding fence device configuration

 Please note that the preceding fencing device is configured to fence only the cluster node called node-1.geekpeek.net.

You must repeat the process of fence device configuration for all cluster nodes, as follows:

```
pcs stonith create ipmilan2 fence_ipmilan ipaddr="192.168.88.101"
login="ipmiuser2" passwd="ipmipass2" action="reboot" pcmk_host_
list="node-2.geekpeek.net"

pcs stonith create ipmilan3 fence_ipmilan ipaddr="192.168.88.102"
login="ipmiuser3" passwd="ipmipass3" action="reboot" pcmk_host_
list="node-3.geekpeek.net"
```

Once configured, the newly configured IPMI management board fencing devices should be listed as stated in the **Full list of resources** that you can see on the screen after running the `pcs status` command:

```
Full list of resources:
 ipmilan1    (stonith:fence_ipmilan):    Started
 ipmilan2    (stonith:fence_ipmilan):    Started
 ipmilan3    (stonith:fence_ipmilan):    Started
```

HP iLO management board fencing

To configure your cluster with HP iLO fencing, you should know the following information:

- **HP iLO address of each cluster node**: This is the IP address of the HP iLO management board. Each cluster node has its own HP iLO IP address.

- **HP iLO login details for each cluster node**: These are the username and password used to successfully connect to the cluster node HP iLO management board. Each cluster node can have different HP iLO login details.

To get information about additional HP iLO fencing agent parameters, run the `pcs stonith describe fence_ilo` command. You can download the output of this command from the `command-5.txt` file from the code bundle.

You can configure an HP iLO management board fencing device with the following command:

```
pcs stonith create hpilo1 fence_ilo ipaddr="192.168.88.100"
login="hpilouser1" passwd="hpilopass1" action="reboot" pcmk_host_
list="node-1.geekpeek.net"
```

Let's take a look at the following terms:

- `hpilo1`: This parameter is the unique name of a fence device
- `fence_ilo`: This parameter is the fence agent to be used
- `ipaddr="192.168.88.100"`: This parameter is the IP address of the HP iLO management board to connect to
- `login="hpilouser1"`: This parameter is the username used when connecting to the HP iLO management board
- `passwd="hpilopass1"`: This parameter is the password used when connecting to the HP iLO management board
- `action="reboot"`: This parameter is the action the fencing mechanism will perform
- `pcmk_host_list="node-1.geekpeek.net"`: This parameter is the cluster node managed by the corresponding fence device configuration

 Note that the preceding fencing device is configured to fence only the cluster node called `node-1.geekpeek.net`.

You must repeat the process of fence device configuration for all cluster nodes, as follows:

```
pcs stonith create hpilo2 fence_ilo ipaddr="192.168.88.101"
login="hpilouser2" passwd="hpilopass2" action="reboot" pcmk_host_
list="node-2.geekpeek.net"

pcs stonith create hpilo3 fence_ilo ipaddr="192.168.88.102"
login="hpilouser3" passwd="hpilopass3" action="reboot" pcmk_host_
list="node-3.geekpeek.net"
```

Once configured, the newly configured HP iLO management board fencing devices should be listed as stated in the following **Full list of resources** that you can see on the screen after running the `pcs status` command:

```
Full list of resources:
  hpilo1   (stonith:fence_ilo):   Started
  hpilo2   (stonith:fence_ilo):   Started
  hpilo3   (stonith:fence_ilo):   Started
```

Fence test

It is very important to test your fencing configuration very thoroughly to make sure that, when there is a problem in the cluster, the fencing mechanism will work as expected and resolve the issue.

The `stonith_admin` command provides a lot of very useful information and fence management features, as follows:

- It lists configured fencing devices for a specific cluster node
- It lists all configured fencing devices in the cluster
- It queries the status of the fencing device

The `stonith_admin` command also enables you to manually trigger fencing of a cluster node.

The syntax used to fence a cluster node is as follows:

```
stonith_admin --fence="clusternode_name"
```

The preceding command will trigger a fencing action as configured on the cluster node provided with the command.

Summary

In this chapter, you learned what fencing is all about. You learned about the fencing devices you can use and how they must be configured. Since a fencing mechanism is an important cluster task that needs to be tested out thoroughly, you were also provided with information on how to test your fencing configuration and manually fence a cluster node for testing purposes. In the next chapter, you will run cluster failover tests for different scenarios.

13

Testing Failover on CentOS 7

In the previous chapters, you learned how to install and configure the cluster software stack on CentOS 7, and also how to configure and manage cluster nodes and cluster resources. In this chapter, you will test the cluster configuration by manually triggering cluster node failure and making sure that the migration of the configured cluster resources and services was successful.

You should run as many tests as possible with different sorts of scenarios before deploying your cluster on the production environment. Only by thoroughly testing your cluster configuration can you make sure that the cluster configuration is working correctly, as expected, and avoid cluster service downtime.

The following failover testing scenarios are performed on virtualized cluster nodes and are therefore limited by the virtualization technology, but these should give you a general idea on how to perform cluster failover tests.

Hardware failure

If your cluster node experiences a CPU, RAM, or motherboard failure, it is an unrecoverable failure and the cluster node will go offline. The cluster fencing mechanism will fence the problematic cluster node to make sure that it is no longer running and prevent the problematic cluster node from accessing the shared cluster storage. If your cluster node experiences disk failure, it should not be affected due to RAID disk redundancy. In the event of a disk failure, the cluster node should still be operational.

The cluster from the following example is configured to provide a **WebSite** resource group that includes a cluster IP address and Apache webserver instance. The **WebSite** resource group is running on the **node-1.geekpeek.net** cluster node. In the following screenshot, you can see the cluster status prior to the hardware failure test:

```
                              root@node-2:~                                x

  File  Edit  View  Search  Terminal  Help
[root@node-2 ~]# pcs status
Cluster name:
Last updated: Wed Feb 25 22:26:24 2015
Last change: Wed Feb 25 22:19:38 2015 via crm_resource on node-2.geekpeek.net
Stack: corosync
Current DC: node-3.geekpeek.net (3) - partition with quorum
Version: 1.1.10-32.el7_0.1-368c726
3 Nodes configured
2 Resources configured


Online: [ node-1.geekpeek.net node-2.geekpeek.net node-3.geekpeek.net ]

Full list of resources:

 Resource Group: WebSite
     ClusterIP  (ocf::heartbeat:IPaddr2):       Started node-1.geekpeek.net
     WebServer  (ocf::heartbeat:apache):        Started node-1.geekpeek.net

PCSD Status:
   192.168.88.10: Online
   192.168.88.20: Online
   192.168.88.30: Online

Daemon Status:
   corosync: active/enabled
   pacemaker: active/enabled
   pcsd: active/enabled
[root@node-2 ~]#
```

You can proceed to simulate the **node-1.geekpeek.net** cluster node's hardware failure. You can do this by cutting off the power of the **node-1.geekpeek.net** cluster node.

Once the cluster node is powered off, check the cluster status to confirm that the **WebSite** resource group was successfully migrated and started on an operational cluster node. In the following screenshot, you can see the cluster status after the hardware failure test:

```
                              root@node-2:~                              ×

 File  Edit  View  Search  Terminal  Help
[root@node-2 ~]# pcs status
Cluster name:
Last updated: Wed Feb 25 22:26:32 2015
Last change: Wed Feb 25 22:19:38 2015 via crm_resource on node-2.geekpeek.net
Stack: corosync
Current DC: node-3.geekpeek.net (3) - partition with quorum
Version: 1.1.10-32.el7_0.1-368c726
3 Nodes configured
2 Resources configured


Online: [ node-2.geekpeek.net node-3.geekpeek.net ]
OFFLINE: [ node-1.geekpeek.net ]

Full list of resources:

 Resource Group: WebSite
     ClusterIP  (ocf::heartbeat:IPaddr2):     Started node-2.geekpeek.net
     WebServer  (ocf::heartbeat:apache):      Started node-2.geekpeek.net

PCSD Status:
  192.168.88.10: Offline
  192.168.88.20: Online
  192.168.88.30: Online

Daemon Status:
  corosync: active/enabled
  pacemaker: active/enabled
  pcsd: active/enabled
[root@node-2 ~]#
```

As you can see, the **node-1.geekpeek.net** cluster node is offline and the **WebSite** resource group was successfully migrated and started on the **node-2.geekpeek.net** cluster node. You can now consider the hardware failure test successful.

Network failure

In the following example, you will perform a cluster node network failure test. Network failure can occur due to network infrastructure equipment failure or cluster node network card failure. It is important to note that the problematic cluster node with network failure could still have access to the shared cluster storage and — therefore — to the cluster data. It is critical for the fencing mechanism to fence the problematic cluster node and make sure that it is offline. In this way, the problematic cluster node can no longer access the cluster data.

The cluster from the following example is configured with a **WebSite** resource group to provide a website cluster service that includes a cluster IP address and an Apache web server instance. The **WebSite** resource group is running on the **node-2. geekpeek.net** cluster node. In the following screenshot, you can see the cluster status prior to the network failure test:

```
                                    root@node-2:~                                   ×

 File  Edit  View  Search  Terminal  Help
[root@node-2 ~]# pcs status
Cluster name:
Last updated: Wed Feb 25 22:36:33 2015
Last change: Wed Feb 25 22:35:37 2015 via crm_resource on node-2.geekpeek.net
Stack: corosync
Current DC: node-3.geekpeek.net (3) - partition with quorum
Version: 1.1.10-32.el7_0.1-368c726
3 Nodes configured
2 Resources configured


Online: [ node-1.geekpeek.net node-2.geekpeek.net node-3.geekpeek.net ]

Full list of resources:

 Resource Group: WebSite
     ClusterIP  (ocf::heartbeat:IPaddr2):       Started node-2.geekpeek.net
     WebServer  (ocf::heartbeat:apache):        Started node-2.geekpeek.net

PCSD Status:
  192.168.88.10: Online
  192.168.88.20: Online
  192.168.88.30: Online

Daemon Status:
  corosync: active/enabled
  pacemaker: active/enabled
  pcsd: active/enabled
[root@node-2 ~]#
```

You can proceed to simulate the **node-2.geekpeek.net** cluster node's network failure by removing the network cables from all the network cards on the **node-2.geekpeek. net** cluster node, and observing the cluster failover process.

Once you have successfully removed the network cables from the network cards, check the cluster status to see whether the **WebSite** resource group was successfully migrated and started on the operational cluster node. In the following screenshot, you can see the cluster status after the network failure test:

```
                              root@node-3:~                              ×

  File  Edit  View  Search  Terminal  Help
[root@node-3 ~]# pcs status
Cluster name:
Last updated: Wed Feb 25 22:37:05 2015
Last change: Wed Feb 25 22:35:37 2015 via crm_resource on node-2.geekpeek.net
Stack: corosync
Current DC: node-3.geekpeek.net (3) - partition with quorum
Version: 1.1.10-32.el7_0.1-368c726
3 Nodes configured
2 Resources configured


Online: [ node-1.geekpeek.net node-3.geekpeek.net ]
OFFLINE: [ node-2.geekpeek.net ]

Full list of resources:

 Resource Group: WebSite
     ClusterIP  (ocf::heartbeat:IPaddr2):        Started node-1.geekpeek.net
     WebServer  (ocf::heartbeat:apache):         Started node-1.geekpeek.net

PCSD Status:
  192.168.88.10: Online
  192.168.88.20: Offline
  192.168.88.30: Online

Daemon Status:
  corosync: active/enabled
  pacemaker: active/enabled
  pcsd: active/enabled
[root@node-3 ~]#
```

As you can see, the **node-2.geekpeek.net** cluster node is offline and the **WebSite** resource group was migrated and successfully started on the **node-1.geekpeek.net** cluster node. You can now consider the network failure test a success.

Summary

In this chapter, you learned that testing your cluster configuration is very important before deploying your cluster on the production environment. You saw how to perform tests of hardware and network failure and how to check whether the test was successful or not. You should come up with additional cluster failover tests to cover as many scenarios as possible. The failover tests depend on the cluster infrastructure and cluster configuration and are specific for every cluster. The cluster administrator should have an idea of which tests should be performed. By thoroughly testing your cluster configuration, you can prevent unwanted cluster service downtime.

14
Two-node Cluster Considerations on CentOS 7

In previous chapters, you learned what high availability is all about and how to achieve it. You also learned how to install and configure a three-node cluster on CentOS 7. A guide to high availability on CentOS 7 cannot be complete without mentioning considerations for a two-node cluster configuration. In this chapter, you will learn the downsides of using a two-node cluster configuration and workarounds for these issues.

Quorum in a two-node cluster

You learned about quorum in *Chapter 2, Meet the Cluster Stack on CentOS*. Quorum is the minimum number of cluster member votes required to perform a cluster operation. Without Quorum, the cluster cannot operate. Quorum is achieved when the majority of cluster members vote to execute a specific cluster operation. If no majority is reached, the cluster operation will not be performed.

You probably see where this is going. In a two-node cluster configuration, the maximum number of expected votes is two—each cluster node has one vote. In a cluster node failure scenario, only one cluster node is active and a cluster node has only one vote. In such a configuration, Quorum cannot be reached because no majority can be delivered. The single cluster node is stuck at 50 percent and will never get past that value. Therefore, the cluster will never operate normally in this way.

The quorum provider in the CentOS 7 cluster stack is Corosync. The CentOS 7 cluster stack, as opposed to the CentOS 6 cluster stack, only provides one option to work around the quorum issue, which is a two-node-specific cluster configuration. The CentOS 7 cluster stack lacks the Quorum disk workaround option, mainly due to the additional Quorum configuration options provided by Corosync version 2. These additional Corosync version 2 options actually make the Quorum disk unnecessary in a two-node or multinode cluster configuration. The new Quorum features of Corosync version 2 are definitely welcome, are well thought out, and can replace the need for a Quorum disk in every way.

Two-node cluster configuration

As already mentioned, the quorum provider in the CentOS 7 cluster stack is Corosync version 2. Therefore, the cluster quorum configuration is provided in the corosync.conf configuration file. With the previous Corosync version (version 1), the quorum capabilities were provided by CMAN; with Corosync version 2 included in the CentOS 7 cluster stack, the quorum capabilities are provided by Corosync itself, specifically by the votequorum process.

If you are configuring a two-node cluster on the CentOS 7 cluster stack, you should enable the two_node cluster option by adding the following parameter to the corosync.conf Quorum section:

two_node: 1

By enabling the two_node cluster option, the quorum is artificially set to 1, which means that the cluster will be quorate and continue to operate even in the event of a failure of one cluster node. Note that enabling the two_node cluster option automatically enables an additional wait_for_all option, which is explained in the following list. You can download an example corosync.conf two-node cluster configuration file with the two_node option enabled from the corosync-conf-1.txt file in the code bundle.

The additional Quorum configuration options in Corosync version 2 are as follows:

- **wait_for_all (default: 0)**: The general behavior of the votequorum process is to switch from inquorate to quorate as soon as possible. As soon as the majority of nodes are visible to each other, the cluster becomes quorate. The wait_for_all option, or WFA, allows you to configure the cluster to become quorate for the first time, but only after all the nodes have become visible. If the two_node option is enabled, the wait_for_all option is automatically enabled as well.

- **last_man_standing (default: 0) / last_man_standing_window (default: 10)**: The general behavior of the `votequorum` process is to set the `expected_votes` parameter and quorum at startup. Enabling the `last_man_standing` option, or `LMS`, allows the cluster to dynamically recalculate the `expected_votes` parameter and quorum under specific circumstances. It is important to enable the `WFA` option when using the `LMS` option in high-availability clusters.

- **auto_tie_breaker (default: 0)**: When the `auto_tie_breaker` option, or `ATB`, is enabled, the cluster can suffer because of up to 50 percent of the nodes failing at the same time. The cluster partition, or the set of nodes that are still in contact with the node that has the lowest `nodeid` parameter, will remain quorate. The other nodes will be inquorate.

 You must always disable fencing in a two-node cluster configuration without the Quorum disk to avoid fence race scenarios, where the two cluster nodes kill each other.

Summary

You have successfully finished the chapters on CentOS 7 cluster installation and configuration. In this chapter, you learned how to prepare the operating system for cluster software; install, configure, and test the cluster software; manage the cluster resources and cluster nodes; and configure fencing and a quorum disk. You should now be able to fully and individually administer a CentOS 7 cluster running on Corosync and Pacemaker.

Index

resource groups
  adding 105
  configuring 112, 113
  removing 119-121
resources
  adding 105
  banning 114-118
  clearing 114-118
  configuring 105-109
  managing 114
  moving 114, 115
  removing 121, 122
  starting 114-117
  start resource, debugging 114
  stopping 114-116
RGManager
  about 20
  cluster service 40
  configuring 36-38, 60
  failover domain 39
  global cluster resources 40
  installing 36-38, 60
  working with 39, 40
Ricci
  configuring 58
  installing 58
ring 12

S

Secure Shell (SSH) 21
SELinux 23
Server Message Block (SMB) 7
server_root option 45

shared storage solution
  about 6
  Distributed Replicated Block Device
    (DRBD) 7
  Network-attached Storage (NAS) 7
  Storage Area Network (SAN) 7
Shoot The Other Node In The
    Head (STONITH)
  about 17, 133
  fencing technique 65
split brain 15
standby mode, cluster node 127-129
Storage Area Network (SAN) 7
system design 3

T

TCP/IP 10
tie-breaker vote 15
Totem Single-ring Ordering and
    Membership (TOTEM) 12-14
two-node cluster
  configuration 82, 150, 151
  quorom 81, 149, 150

U

UDP/IP 10

Z

Zabbix 3
Zenoss 3

Thank you for buying
CentOS High Availability

About Packt Publishing

Packt, pronounced 'packed', published its first book, *Mastering phpMyAdmin for Effective MySQL Management*, in April 2004, and subsequently continued to specialize in publishing highly focused books on specific technologies and solutions.

Our books and publications share the experiences of your fellow IT professionals in adapting and customizing today's systems, applications, and frameworks. Our solution-based books give you the knowledge and power to customize the software and technologies you're using to get the job done. Packt books are more specific and less general than the IT books you have seen in the past. Our unique business model allows us to bring you more focused information, giving you more of what you need to know, and less of what you don't.

Packt is a modern yet unique publishing company that focuses on producing quality, cutting-edge books for communities of developers, administrators, and newbies alike. For more information, please visit our website at www.packtpub.com.

About Packt Open Source

In 2010, Packt launched two new brands, Packt Open Source and Packt Enterprise, in order to continue its focus on specialization. This book is part of the Packt Open Source brand, home to books published on software built around open source licenses, and offering information to anybody from advanced developers to budding web designers. The Open Source brand also runs Packt's Open Source Royalty Scheme, by which Packt gives a royalty to each open source project about whose software a book is sold.

Writing for Packt

We welcome all inquiries from people who are interested in authoring. Book proposals should be sent to author@packtpub.com. If your book idea is still at an early stage and you would like to discuss it first before writing a formal book proposal, then please contact us; one of our commissioning editors will get in touch with you.

We're not just looking for published authors; if you have strong technical skills but no writing experience, our experienced editors can help you develop a writing career, or simply get some additional reward for your expertise.

CentOS System Administration Essentials

ISBN: 978-1-78398-592-0   Paperback: 174 pages

Become an efficient CentOS administrator by acquiring real-world knowledge of system setup and configuration

1. Centralize user accounts in openLDAP and understand how Directory can be at the back-end of many services.

2. Learning Puppet to centralize server configuration will free up your time as configuration is handled just once on the configuration server.

3. A step-by-step guide that covers the very popular Linux Distribution CentOS 6.5 with easy-to-follow instructions.

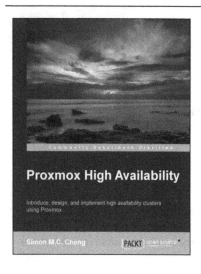

Proxmox High Availability

ISBN: 978-1-78398-088-8   Paperback: 258 pages

Introduce, design, and implement high availability clusters using Proxmox

1. Plan and construct a high availability environment from scratch using Proxmox.

2. Migrate current systems to high availability clusters to improve the level of service availability.

3. A step-by-step guide to disaster recovery, on failed high availability clusters.

Please check **www.PacktPub.com** for information on our titles

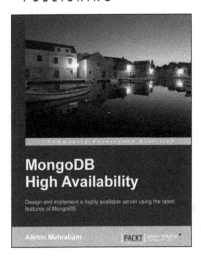

MongoDB
High Availability

Design and implement a highly available server using the latest features of MongoDB

Afshin Mehrabani   PACKT | open source ✲

MongoDB High Availability

ISBN: 978-1-78398-672-9   Paperback: 164 pages

Design and implement a highly available server using the latest features of MongoDB

1. Improve response time by profiling and indexing on large databases.

2. Configure a Replica set network from scratch using a real-world example.

3. Step-by-step guide to setting up and learning about the latest MongoDB components and features to perform clustering and sharding.

Cassandra High
Availability

Harness the power of Apache Cassandra to build scalable, fault-tolerant, and readily available applications

Robbie Strickland   PACKT | open source ✲

Cassandra High Availability

ISBN: 978-1-78398-912-6   Paperback: 186 pages

Harness the power of Apache Cassandra to build scalable, fault-tolerant, and readily available applications

1. Master the essentials behind building highly available applications on top of Apache Cassandra.

2. Learn how to effectively configure and deploy Apache Cassandra across multiple data centers.

3. Avoid common pitfalls that prevent applications from achieving 100 percent uptime.

Please check **www.PacktPub.com** for information on our titles

www.ingramcontent.com/pod-product-compliance
Lightning Source LLC
Chambersburg PA
CBHW060136060326
40690CB00018B/3902